Research Methodology for Computer Science

Computing and classification of sciences

Ayden Melton

2

Contents

Computing and Classification of Sciences

Computing is sometimes classified among the exact sciences, sometimes among Engineering, but some of its subareas are very close to the social and human sciences. Proceedings of events in distinct subareas are so different from each other that sometimes a member of one subarea has difficulty understanding the jargon or even the methodology of the other subarea. Exact or inexact science, hard or soft, empirical or formal. This chapter analyzes Computing in the light of classifications of the sciences, aiming to enlighten its practitioners about the richness and variety of this area of research.

This chapter is a reflection, and there is no pretense that this is a complete and definitive study on the subject. The aim is to explore and raise questions, and to reflect on them rather than answer them.

2.1 Science and its Classifications

One can understand that science is the effort to discover and increase human knowledge of how reality works and could work. Thus, the term "science" excludes several human activities, such as technological development, since it does not necessarily seek explanations, but solutions.

One of the usual tools of scientists is analysis, through which the universe can be divided and, in this way, its parts explained in a more understandable way. Thus, given the variety of approaches, several classifications of the sciences were produced in an attempt to better understand their methods and objectives. This chapter addresses some of these classifications and seeks to show which subareas of Computing fall into one or the other.

One of the best-known criteria for classifying the sciences is the one that distinguishes the sciences into formal and empirical (Morris, 1935). It can be said that formal sciences study ideas, while empirical sciences study things.

The formal sciences, then, study ideas independently of their application to nature or to human beings. This does not mean that they cannot be applied, and they usually are, but the object of study of these sciences is in the form, that is, in the purely logical or mathematical processes.

Logic, Mathematics, Microeconomics, Statistics and the formal aspects of Linguistics are cited among the formal sciences. Among the subareas of Computing, there are several that correspond predominantly to the formal sciences: the theory of algorithms, involving programming techniques, data structures, complexity and decidability, the theory of formal languages, used in the construction of compilers, the formal aspects of artificial intelligence, relational calculus in database, etc.

Empirical sciences are also sometimes called real or factual sciences. They study phenomena that occur in the real world and that, therefore, are not merely formal. They must make use of observations to substantiate their findings. In the empirical sciences, a pretty theory that is not supported by observations is worthless.

The empirical sciences can still be divided into two groups: those that study nature, or natural sciences, and those that study the human being and its interactions, or social sciences (Hempel, 1965).

The natural sciences study the universe in its aspects that are independent of the existence or action of the human being. Among them are astronomy, physics, chemistry, biology and earth sciences. The aspects of Computing related to the natural sciences are usually related to the hardware of the machines that perform computations. Electronics, logic circuits, processors, in short, all the physical components of a computer are studied as natural phenomena. A Turing machine (Turing, 1937), for example, is an ideal processor, with infinite memory, and is studied in the Theory of Computation as a formal artifact. Real processors have physical limitations of space, speed, heat and power consumption; thus, they are studied as natural phenomena.

The social sciences study aspects of human relationships, that is, the social life of individuals. Among the social sciences are Anthropology, Communication, Economics, History, Politics, Psychology and Sociology, among others.

The sub-areas of Computing closest to the social sciences are software engineering, informatics in education, electronic commerce systems, certain aspects of artificial intelligence, which studies the social interactions of multi-agent systems based on observations of human behavior in society. etc.

Thus, it is observed that, given this form of classification of the sciences, there are subareas of Computing in all of them. Not to mention the multidisciplinary areas, which effectively interact Computing with other sciences, such as Economics, Medicine, Geography, etc. There are both situations in which Computing is applied to promote studies in other areas, as in the case of georeferencing systems, as well as situations in which knowledge from other areas is applied in Computing, as in the case of neural networks and genetic algorithms, both computational mechanisms Inspired by Biology.

Scientific computing, or computational science, is still considered a third mode of science, complementing theory and experimentation. Scientific computing is based on the construction of mathematical models and their simulation on computers to solve problems in related areas, such as Physics, Chemistry, Biology, etc.

It is interesting to note that formal sciences also admit formal proofs. Two plus two is four, and that doesn't change! Empirical sciences, on the other hand, seek explanations (theories) that best explain observations. For example, why is the sky blue? Why do birds migrate? Why does a programmer on an agile team produce more quality? Different answers can be given to these questions, but hardly one of them will be definitive. The answers (theories) are assumed to be valid while better answers are not found. In this aspect, the empirical sciences are in constant revision. And this is part of the process of seeking knowledge.

2.3 Pure and Applied Sciences

Another classification of the sciences derives from the way in which their studies are applied. According to this classification, there are pure and applied sciences (Gregory, 1942).

The pure sciences, or fundamental sciences, study the basic concepts of knowledge without concern for their immediate application. This is not to say that they are not empirical sciences. They can be empirical or formal. Pure here means being more interested in the foundations, the laws that govern physical phenomena or ideas. Cosmology is considered a pure science par excellence, since it studies the formation of the Universe without explicit concern with practical applications. But cosmology is also an empirical science, because its theories need to be validated by observing phenomena. In some cases, phenomena were observed before a coherent theory existed, as in the case of the motion of stars and planets. In other cases, the theory arose before the phenomenon was observed, as in the case of black holes,

Logic, on the other hand, can also be considered a pure and formal science, since it studies the relationships between ideas and not between physical things.

The pure science aspect of Computing is difficult to identify, as most Computing results have practical application. So maybe this aspect is more linked to the researcher's intention than to a specific subarea. A clear example of pure research that only came to produce practical applications later was Chaos Theory (Kellert, 1993), which evolved from observations of phenomena obtained with computational tools.

Another subarea of Computing that has a strong characteristic of pure science is the study of multi-agent systems and also the area known as computational mathematics (Self, 1995), that is, the study of human learning simulated by computers. The objective of these subareas is usually to understand how social or learning processes occur among human beings from the elaboration and testing of computational models that incorporate theories that try to explain some phenomena.

Applied sciences, on the other hand, aim at making discoveries that can be immediately applied to some industrial or similar process to produce some kind of gain. Engineering, in general, can be classified under this classification.

Computing is often seen as an engineering discipline. There is software engineering, computer engineering and computer engineering, each with a different objective, but all have in common the production of knowledge for application in software, systems or hardware production processes.

Applied science is often confused with technology. But, as will be seen later, they are different things.

2.4 Exact and Inexact Sciences

Another classification characterizes the sciences as exact and inexact (Helmer and Rescher, 1959). Computer Science is usually classified among the exact sciences, but some subfields can have totally different characteristics.

The exact sciences are those whose results are precise. Its laws are highly predictive and predictable. Experiments can be repeated over and over again, yielding the same or statistically predictable results. Mathematics par excellence are classified among the exact sciences, but also Physics, Chemistry and parts of some natural and social sciences.

Inexact sciences are those that can predict general behavior of their phenomena, but whose results are not always as expected. This is usually because it is very difficult to evaluate all the data that produce the results. Inexact sciences include Meteorology, Economics, and most of the social sciences.

Computing, like the other exact sciences, also has inexact aspects. Genetic algorithms and some neural network models are capable of producing unexpected results even when applied repeatedly to the same dataset.

Computing techniques are also applied to make predictions in many areas, with results that are not always exact.

A classification, perhaps less well known, divides the sciences into hard and soft (Hedges, 1987). This classification is related to the rigor of the method used.

The hard sciences would be those that use scientific rigor in their observations, experiments and deductions. When the hard sciences are formal, they heavily use Logic and Mathematics as theoretical construction tools. The hard natural sciences often rely on statistical evidence to give credibility to their experiments. Medical research can be classified in this sense as a hard natural science, as it requires great rigor in proving empirical results.

Soft sciences, on the other hand, tend to accept evidence based on anecdotal data, that is, on case studies. This occurs when it is difficult or impossible to carry out fully controlled experiments.

In general, Computing is understood to be a hard science, but the reality, in many cases, is that researchers have difficulty providing enough data to empirically support their conclusions. Thus, we still see many articles in Computing that use one or a few case studies to try to "validate" a technique, model or theory. As seen below, the case study is an excellent source of data for exploratory research, but, unless there is a contradiction in a commonly accepted theory, the case study does not validate the hypothesis being studied.

2.6 Nomothetic and Idiographic Sciences

The vast majority of sciences are nomothetic, since these sciences study phenomena that are repeated and that can lead to the discovery of general laws that allow predictions to be made.

But some sciences are idiographic, as they analyze unique phenomena that do not repeat themselves, but which nevertheless have validity as a field of study (Windelband, 1980).

History is the great example of idiographic science, since the facts do not repeat themselves and it is extremely difficult, if not impossible, to find sufficiently deterministic patterns in History that allow making predictions from observations. In science fiction, however, this has already been predicted (Asimov, 2019).

In Computing, few subfields are idiographic. In particular, the study of the history of Computing and the development of companies or certain technologies, such as languages, paradigms and computational architectures, can be seen in this way.

Scientific Method

Several philosophical currents influenced what is now known as science. These currents are analyzed in this chapter.

The scientific method is particularly important in computing because, as an empirical science, it cannot just be concerned with collecting data. Explanation of the data is much more important.

It is not enough, for example, to prove the effectiveness of a system, to apply it in two groups, one of test (A) and one of control (B), and to conclude that the average of group A was greater than the average of the group B. First, because it would be necessary to demonstrate that the difference between the means is not just a result of chance. Once, a student applied a questionnaire to five people (real case). Three answered "yes", and two, "no". The student concluded that there was a tendency for "yes" (60% of "yes" answers). But what value is this conclusion? Could he publish the results of an electoral opinion poll, for example, based on five interviews?

Even considering that the difference between the two means is significant, this finding will have little value without a theory that explains the reason for this difference.

If one group used educational software and another did not, and the educational software group scored better, what does that prove? Could it be that the software has improved learning? Yes. But it could also be that the students who used the software simply studied more because they were ashamed of getting lower grades than the others who did not use the software. It could also be that the group that did not use the software felt discredited and was less interested in the subject.

That is, several explanations may exist. It is up to the researcher to discover the most likely according to the scientific method.

3.1 Empiricism

A saying has become a classic in computing: "Theory is when the phenomenon is understood, but it doesn't work; practice is when it works, but you don't know why. In Computing, theory and practice coexist: nothing works and no one knows why." This practice has been one of the meanings adopted for the term "empirical" by developers in the area of Computing. It doesn't matter why, it just works. If it works it's right! This pragmatic point of view, however, does not correspond to the meaning of "empirical" given by science. According to Kerlinger (1980), "empirical means guided by the evidence obtained in systematic and controlled scientific research".

Thus, by seeking concrete and repeatable evidence and not just opinions or superstitions, perhaps empiricism was the most important of all influences on the scientific method.

John Locke (1632-1704) is considered the first empiricist philosopher. He established that every scientific theory must be based on observations that can be tested and produce general laws with predictive power. In this way, scientific theories can be verified in the light of empirical evidence and, when they do not adequately explain the observable facts, they must be refuted.

It is common to find "studies" on the internet that point out the most miraculous and simple home remedies that the evil industry doesn't want you to know. But the fact that one or two people drank lemon juice in the morning and cured their migraines does not mean that this is empirical evidence. Just like an extremely cold day in your city's winter doesn't mean that average global temperatures aren't rising over the decades. Isolated cases and outliers are not enough scientific evidence to prove laws of cause and effect, such as that lemon juice cures migraines, even if it worked for your aunt.

Computing, as a science, bases its research on empiricism and not on the principle of authority. In Computing, most of the time, the opinion of this or that exponent matters little, but the objective conclusions obtained empirically.

Lack of empiricism can lead to wrong conclusions. In the Middle Ages, men were believed to have one less rib than women, as the Bible reports that women were created from a man's rib. This belief could easily be refuted if one were to use empiricism to simply count the number of ribs in either sex.

Descartes (2004) believed that the heart beat because it was the hottest place in the body, and its heat inflated the blood that entered it. This conclusion, reached with some reflection, but little empirical evidence, is of no use today, at least in the field of Medicine.

Empiricism is important to science, therefore, because it is a sensible way of looking at the world. It is not enough to believe in your intuition or in the words of the masters. It is necessary to objectively verify if the phenomenon described is in fact true. Some modern and ancient theories, generally explored by some guru, are considered pseudosciences because their explanations do not find empirical support. Examples of pseudosciences are parapsychology, astrology, ufology, numerology, flat earth theory, homeopathy, among others.

One student wrote early on in his article: "Most programmers don't like to use UML." But is this empirically based or is it just his feeling? Will it be true? Who said? How did he observe this fact? This simple information may even be true, but what are the empirical data that support the claim? Where do the numbers come from? Without that, it's just his personal opinion.

These doubts are important for the scientist who really wants to understand phenomena and discover new knowledge. If doctors today continued to believe that the heart beats because it warms the blood, based on Descartes' assertion, very few advances in Medicine would have been achieved. Doubting the conclusions of other scientists and doubting one's own common sense is often the key to great discoveries.

3.2 Positivism

Positivism proposes that science should be based only on human values, leaving theology, mysticism and metaphysics in another sphere that should not interfere with scientific observations and theories.

Auguste Comte (1798-1857) is considered the founder of sociology and positivism. According to him, science does not peremptorily deny most popular beliefs, whether religious or not. But until such beliefs are tested by the scientific method, science can say nothing about them. That is, science has not yet proved that angels exist, but neither has it proved that they do not exist. So she says nothing about them.

On the other hand, positivism often leads to reductionism, that is, to the belief that a phenomenon can be divided into its components, and these components studied individually under controlled conditions. This can often be the case. But in some situations it is difficult to remove a phenomenon from its context and analyze it in a controlled laboratory situation. For example, in software quality, one can easily analyze the internal and external qualities in a laboratory environment. Examples of these qualities are maintainability, testability, time efficiency, usability, among others. But the qualities of the software in use, according to the ISO 25010 Standard, can only be evaluated with the product being used in its real environment. Assessing one of these qualities, for example, requires checking whether the software is making a profit, reducing expenses or mitigating risks to the organization where it is used. How to assess this in a controlled laboratory environment?

Thus, positivism can be applied in scientific studies as long as one is convinced that the phenomenon can be studied isolated from its context. Otherwise, other principles, still to be commented, may be necessary.

3.3 Pragmatism

Pragmatism is a philosophical current that opposes scientific realism. Realists hold that science does describe reality. Pragmatists, on the other hand, assume that it is not possible to know exactly what reality is and that, thus, science explains only observed phenomena, and its predictions are consistent and useful. John Dewey (1859-1952) was a philosopher with great influence on pragmatic thinking.

One thing most empirical scientists do not admit is absolute knowledge. Every theory, every explanation related to the observed phenomena, is always accepted because it is consistent with the latter. But every theory is liable to be contradicted or refuted by new observations that are not consistent with it. Even the most fundamental explanations can be refuted if they are not consistent with empirical observations. This is because science, according to pragmatism, does not make statements about nature as it is, but about our observations about nature.

A scientist must always be attentive to the results of his observations. In Computing, as in other areas, finding phenomena that do not fit the currently accepted explanations can be the key to great discoveries.

For a pragmatist, knowledge is judged on the basis of its usefulness. That is, scientific truth consists of what in practice is working and serves some purpose. So pragmatism can also lead to relativism, since something that is useful to one person may not be useful to another.

3.4 Objectivity

Another obvious feature of the scientific method is objectivity, that is, the possibility that any two people with an acceptable level of competence can reach the same conclusions when analyzing the data.

The criterion of objectivity, therefore, leaves out opinions in science because opinions are subjective and depend on the experience, character and motivation of the people who express them. For example, a programmer might claim that functional programming is better than imperative programming. But without an objective measure that quantitatively defines what it means to be "better", this opinion could be challenged by other programmers. The clash of opinions can even be healthy, but it is difficult to do science with subjective issues, such as judgment or preferences.

Computing also does not base its research on the principle of authority. So, perhaps, articles published in Computing make little use of citations of opinions from classical authorities. This is more common in the area of law. Usually, articles in Computing present concepts obtained in the literature, related works, among the most recent, and an objective work, empirically evaluated.

In addition, a very healthy principle in research is to make critical readings, even of the most consecrated works. A reading with the sole purpose of learning can be positive, but a critical reading, in which one doubts, at first, what the author says, can generate much more research ideas.

According to Kerlinger (1980), "the main condition for satisfying the criterion of objectivity is, ideally, that any observers with a minimum of competence agree with their results".

It is still possible to define a phenomenon objectively, but in a diffuse way, that is, instead of working with just two categories such as "easy" or "difficult", one works with an inherent degree of difficulty. Again, the objective definition must consider a measurement that can be performed independently by different observers and still arrive at the same results. Building on the previous example, then, it would be possible to define the degree of difficulty as the average time that users with a certain degree of training take to perform a set of tasks previously defined using the tool. In this case, several measurements will reach objective values, and comparisons can be made between the systems.

However, having an objective definition of a phenomenon is not enough to produce quality work. It is also necessary to observe the quality of the definition itself. That is, there may be researchers who do not agree that the average time to perform a set of tasks is a good definition for "ease of use". Taking the case to an extreme for better understanding, if a researcher were to define that a system is easy to use just based on his subjective opinion, that definition will hardly be accepted.

So, to work with observations of phenomena, the researcher must objectively define the phenomenon that he is going to observe and convince others that this definition is reasonably intuitive, but especially useful, to reach some result.

3.5 Induction

The scientific method also presents as one of its principles that a situation that holds in all observed cases holds in all cases, until proven otherwise. This is known as the induction principle (Vickers, 2006).

There is no a priori reason to believe that laws induced from repeated observations have exceptions, unless that exception is actually observed or that some other knowledge might point to the possibility of its existence. For example, as flying horses have never been observed (at least by reliable sources) and there is no knowledge that could indicate their existence, there is no reason to believe that they exist.

This is not to say that if a person has only seen white swans, there are no black swans. This person may initially accept the fact that all swans are white, but if he comes into contact with a black swan he should immediately abandon this theory.

Thus, natural induction can only be applied as a scientific principle when it is effectively consistent with other knowledge and observations made.

Depending on the property evaluated, however, some care must be taken, as some of them are diffuse (Zadeh, 1965). For example, a newborn child can be assumed to be young. If a person is young, it is assumed that adding one day to his age will not make him stop being young. Thus, it is concluded that people of any age are young. The flaw in this reasoning lies in the definition of "being young", which is diffuse, that is, with each added day it gets a little less young.

Structural induction (Burstall, 1969) is a more general case, of which mathematical induction is a particular case. Structural induction is necessary when there is more than one rule to form elements.

This principle can be applied, among other things, in formal software specification. If an object is created consistently with its specification, and if operations that change that object preserve its specification, the object will always be consistent.

3.6 Refutation

The principle of refutation (Popper, 1959) or contradiction of a theory states that any scientific theory that seeks to explain observable facts is always open to being invalidated if it is not able to explain new observables.

A case study, as exploratory research, for example, cannot prove a general rule, but it can prove that a commonly accepted general rule is not fully valid. This happens if the case study points to a situation in which the rule does not present the expected result. In particular, the case study should already have some hypothesis to be analyzed in advance, so that the researcher can carry it out with an objective in mind.

The fact that new observables are found unexplained by the general law does not necessarily mean that the law should be completely discarded. For example, despite the Theory of Relativity, Newton's physics still explains very well the phenomena that occur on the surface of the Earth. Thus, when new observables contradict a theory, one can either discard the original theory, replacing it with an entirely new one, or differentiate the original theory into two theories with applications in specific sub-cases.

The principle of coherentism (Joachim, 1906) is highly connected with the philosophy of pragmatism. So, at no time will the scientist claim that his theory explains reality. He can only assert that his theory is consistent with the observations and that, by the principle of induction, in the absence of refutation this theory can be accepted as an explanation.

Coherentism avoids the problem of Descartes' (2004) criterion, whereby any claim needs to be justified on the basis of other claims, leading to an infinite regress. With coherentism, what is expected is not that every statement has an explanation, but that it is coherent with a previously accepted system of knowledge.

3.8 Occam's Blade

One question that would go unanswered without Occam's blade principle (Ockham, 1495) is the fact that any finite set of observables can have infinite explanatory theories, especially if variations between theories cannot be immediately empirically tested. For example, the theory that the acceleration due to gravity is about 9.8 m/s2 can have infinite variations if additions are introduced such as "except January 10, 2070, when it will be 9.6 m/s2". As it is not possible to test this theory before 2070, both it and the more commonly accepted law would be equally plausible explanations.

But the principle of Occam's blade says that in the case of several theories that explain the same observations, the simplest of them should be preferred. W. Ockham's original statement would have been: "Numquam ponenda est pluralitas sine necessitate", that is, never use more than is really necessary. In the previous example, the alternative theory cannot be tested before 2070, but the addition it places on the general theory is gratuitous and has no basis in any plausible explanation or cause. Furthermore, it is not consistent with observations and general knowledge about how gravity works.

Without a rule like Occam's blade, science would not be possible. However, sometimes this rule can be misused. It does not say that the simplest explanation is always preferable. In fact, the simplest explanation among those that effectively explain the observables should be preferred over others.

3.9 Constructivism

Another current of thought that influences scientific research is constructivism. Constructivism seeks to go beyond reductionism and positivism, claiming that not only elaborate scientific truths, but all meanings in general, are collectively constructed by Humanity. Thus, laboratory experiments under controlled conditions may not represent all the nuances and complexity of the real world.

Researchers with constructivist convictions are unlikely to carry out controlled reductionist experiments; they will prefer action research or ethnography or even case studies to build their theories.

Since individual observations and social interactions count for a lot for constructivism, researchers will often be more interested in discovering local theories than general theories, i.e., different individuals will be able to attribute different meanings to the same phenomena, as the phenomena need to fit their own. local or particular theories.

Although some constructivist ideas had already been proposed by philosophers since Ancient Greece, the term only takes on the meaning we assign today from the work of Jean Piaget (1896-1980).

Search Types

The term "research" can refer to a variety of human activities, ranging from conducting electoral polls to scientific research that seeks to increase human knowledge about how the world works or could work.

Research, in the scientific context, can be classified according to different criteria. Research work is not always limited to a single type. Also, some types of research can be the basis for others.

In this chapter, scientific research is characterized in relation to its nature, objectives and technical procedures. In addition, the end of the chapter presents a discussion of the differences between science and technology and their interconnections.

4.1 Regarding Nature

As for the nature of the research, it can be differentiated into primary, secondary and tertiary.

Primary research seeks to present new knowledge from observations and theories built to explain them. New information is assumed to be relevant when it has implications for the way processes and systems are understood or when it has practical implications for their realization. Thus, primary or original research consists of carrying out experiments, interviews, observations, etc. for any new information to be discovered.

Secondary or bibliographic research seeks to obtain information only on previously published works. There are at least two usual forms of secondary research: systematic literature mapping and systematic literature review. The main objective of mapping is usually to increase the understanding of an area of knowledge, offering an overview of the research, indicating its evolution and current state. The systematic review, on the other hand, has more specific objectives, seeking to answer research questions with data and results from published works.

When a certain area of knowledge already has a significant number of published secondary research, it is still possible to start with tertiary research, that is, a systematic review on systematic reviews.

Both primary and secondary and tertiary research are only interesting if they effectively answer some research question. Carrying out a literature mapping just to produce statistical graphs with no conclusions will be of little value. Chapter 8 goes into more detail about writing good research questions.

4.2 Regarding the Objectives

Regarding the objectives, the research can be exploratory, descriptive, explanatory or design.

Exploratory research is research in which the author does not necessarily have a definite hypothesis or goal in mind. It can often be considered the first stage of a longer research process. In exploratory research, the author will examine a set of phenomena, looking for known or unknown anomalies that can then be the basis for more systematic research later.

Descriptive research is more objective than exploratory. With it, we seek to obtain more consistent data about a given reality, but there is still no interference from the researcher or the attempt to obtain theories that explain the phenomena. One only tries to describe the facts as they are or to categorize them. Descriptive research is characterized by data collection and the application of interviews and questionnaires. Like exploratory research, it can be considered a previous step to find phenomena not explained by current theories.

Explanatory research is the most complex and complete. It is scientific research par excellence because, in addition to analyzing the observed data, it seeks its causes and explanations, that is, the determining factors of these data.

While exploratory, descriptive and explanatory research seeks to understand things as they are, design or project research is an attempt to determine how things could be. For example, a researcher is not only interested in knowing which is the best tool to carry out a certain activity, he wants to find out what the ideal tool would look like, which possibly does not yet exist.

4.3 Regarding the Technical Procedures

As for the technical procedures, the research can be classified as bibliographical, documentary, experimental, survey, action research, ethnographic or case study, among other forms. In addition, mixed techniques are often applied, especially combining bibliographic research with other forms.

This type of research is carried out on indexed documents such as journals, conference proceedings, monographs, technical reports, etc.

Documentary research, on the other hand, consists of analyzing documents or data that have not yet been systematized and published. You can examine company reports, files obtained from public agencies, databases, correspondence, etc. That is, documentary research seeks to find information and patterns in documents not yet treated systematically. Searching for patterns in requirements documents prepared by software development companies would be an example of desk research in Computing.

Experimental research is characterized by the manipulation of an aspect of reality by the researcher. The researcher introduces, for example, a new technique in a software company and observes if the productivity increases. Experimental research implies having one or more experimental variables that can be controlled by the researcher (whether or not he uses a certain technique, for example), and one or more observed variables, the measurement of which could possibly lead to the conclusion that there is some type of dependency with the experimental variable (for example, evaluating the productivity of programmers in function points per working day and verifying whether the technique significantly increases this value).

Experimental research must use rigorous sampling techniques and hypothesis testing so that its results are statistically acceptable and generalizable (Barbetta, Reis and Bornia, 2008).

In some areas of Computing, it is difficult to carry out experimental research, either because of the difficulty in manipulating or measuring the variables, or because of the time that interventions can take. In these cases, survey research can be carried out, whereby existing data will be sought directly in the environment, through observations, measurements, questionnaires and interviews. Once this information is tabulated, conclusions can be drawn about causes and effects.

Basically, non-experimental or observational research consists of the study of phenomena without the systematic intervention of the researcher. For example, a researcher who studies the day-to-day life of a software development company to detect certain practices previously cataloged there is doing non-experimental research, as he only acts by observing and drawing conclusions from a preconceived theoretical framework.

Experimental research, on the other hand, implies that the researcher will systematically cause changes in the environment to be researched, in order to observe whether each intervention produces the expected results.

In the previous example, if the researcher decides to artificially create stressful situations within the company to see how employees react, he will be conducting experimental research. Thus, experimental research is usually linked to the positivist view of science, in which complex reality is reduced to controlled and replicable experiments.

Survey research is usually done with the application of questionnaires to a group of people so that their opinions and observations on a given topic can be better known. It can be used, for example, to find out which techniques and tools have been used in industry or academia and how these techniques and tools are evaluated by these users.

The biggest challenge for survey research is with regard to sample bias. If the researcher wants to know how users rate, for example, tools from company X and does this survey with the employees of company X, he will probably get answers with a more positive bias than if he did the survey in other companies unrelated to X. This may be an extreme case, but more subtle ones are no less problematic for bias.

Action research (Lewin, 1946) is less common in computing, but possible. In it, the researcher interacts with the researched, getting involved in the research work in a participatory way, seeking a certain result.

Action research usually focuses on design, that is, it is not done just to find out what the world is like, but possible interventions to solve unsolved problems.

Action research demands the existence of a problem owner, that is, the "owner" of a problem. This person will engage in research with the aim of solving the problem. It must be evaluated if the problem is relevant and if it does not already have a known solution. For example, a company that delivers buggy software products has a problem. But it's not necessarily a research problem because it's possible that implementing best practices like automated testing, version control, frequent integrations and fast deliveries could solve the company's current problems. Thus, no new knowledge would be generated. On the other hand, a company that has applied many of the known good practices and still faces problems can be an interesting case to study:

Ethnographic research occurs when the researcher actually dives into a social group to observe their behaviors. It is strongly associated with the current of constructivism. For example, a researcher might have observed in a company that different agile teams use different bug reporting tools.

An ethnographic research could be done, in this case, to verify if the teams actually have different needs that are met by different tools or if their needs converge, and also in this way they could converge to an ideal tool. To reach one of these conclusions, the process could then include a period of observation of the work of the different teams while collecting data on the bug report activities and any difficulties faced.

The case study is a technique widely used in Computing, although much confusion still exists in relation to it. First, it should be mentioned that there are two basic types of case studies: exploratory and confirmatory.

In the exploratory case study, the researcher will study in depth some situation, such as the functioning of an agile team, to observe problems and behaviors and possibly develop hypotheses for further study.

The confirmatory case study, or proof of concept, is done to show that in practice a certain theory is effectively confirmed. The confirmatory case study is much more useful for refuting than for confirming theories, since a case in which the theory does not work is enough for it to need to be reformulated. A case study in which the theory works, while it is evidence of validity, is not necessarily proof of validity.

An advantage of case studies in relation to experiments is that they suffer less from the issue of reductionism, since in these cases the researcher effectively observes the phenomenon occurring in the field.

One can also speak of mixed approaches to research, combining two or more of the techniques seen in this section. A very popular technique is triangulation in which the researcher looks for evidence using different techniques. For example, a researcher interested in understanding problems in the agile culture in a given organization can carry out a survey survey (interviews) with developers and then carry out an ethnographic research to verify that, on a day-to-day basis, the answers given actually correspond to reality.

4.4 Science and Technology

In computing, the terms science and technology almost always go so closely together that many people find it difficult to distinguish them. However, science is the search for knowledge and explanations. Science builds theories to explain observed facts. Technology, on the other hand, is the application of knowledge in practical activities, such as industrial and economic activities.

Unlike science, technology is not intended to explain the world. It is practical and exists to transform the world, not to theorize about it.

It is observed that, sometimes, dissertations and theses in Computing, as well as scientific articles, are still strongly characterized as merely technological presentations: systems, prototypes, frameworks, architectures, models, processes, all these constructions are technical, and not necessarily science. .

For a work to be effectively of a scientific nature, it is necessary that the information contained therein explains a little more about why things work as they do or how they could work better. So science can be present in ideas presented in a work. Usually, there is a research problem identified for which a satisfactory solution is not yet known. There is also a hypothesis, that is, an idea that can be tested to solve the problem in whole or in part. The work must show that the idea in question is in fact valid, employing the constructions of the scientific method that apply to the case.

The work can be filled with evidence that in fact new knowledge is being presented. Among these evidences, case studies, comparative bibliographic research, experimental research, etc. can be mentioned. In addition, it is also usually demonstrated that new ideas have practical application in a tool, algorithm, prototype, process, etc. In this way, these artifacts can and should be presented as elements in which the idea is incorporated, gaining life and practical application, that is, fulfilling its technical vocation. The monograph or article should usually not be about the artifact, but about the ideas embodied in it.

At the undergraduate, master's and doctoral levels, research in Computer Science, whatever the subarea, should lead the researcher to seek a contribution to knowledge and not just present new technologies. Although these are also relevant and important, they are not necessarily science, and are therefore suitable only at the undergraduate and specialization levels of work.

Scientific research must be carried out in accordance with the principles of the scientific method. Observations and experiments, if any, must be obtained in a rigorous and repeatable manner. Scientific initiation, master's and doctoral works must, therefore, produce science to be considered scientific research.

Usually, a scientific work is structured around a research problem to be solved (a question not yet satisfactorily answered) and a hypothesis (a possible answer to be evaluated). If the hypothesis is confirmed by empirical or formal evidence, the scientist must present a theory that explains that fact, usually as an extension or alternative to a previous theory.

A successful research will possibly start with an adequate literature review so that the main concepts of the area are known and the latest developments in the area are known. After this review, when the researcher is able to recognize the important questions not yet answered, he can carry out the research work starting, for example, with a case study so that the exploratory research can bring to light new questions and problems. After formulating a hypothesis to solve the indicated problem and a justification that explains why the hypothesis should work, the researcher can apply the appropriate empirical methods to convince others that his hypothesis is correct according to the principles of the scientific method, that is, ,

Scientific research cannot be defined as a cake recipe, in which the same sequence of steps must always be carried out to reach the expected result, but it is imagined that it follows certain criteria so that it is objective, that is, so that others accept their results as valid regardless of opinion or preference.

Research Maturity

It is often said that Computing or Informatics is a new area in the field of science and that it is in full development. But this does not justify that the scientific method used in the area of Computing has to be vague and that so many monographs are written with a weak methodological basis.

This discrepancy in research styles and low conformation to scientific methodology happens not only because the area is new, but also because Computing permeates practically all human activities and, therefore, is interrelated with many other disciplines.

The very observation of the emergence of the first Computer Science courses in Brazil is evidence of this variety of approaches and interrelationships. Some courses appeared in the faculties of Engineering. In other universities, courses in Computing came from the faculties of Mathematics or Physics. In some cases, Computing courses emerged from data processing departments whose purpose was to provide services and not teaching.

The variety of courses, and even denominations, caused great confusion on the national scene until approximately the year 2000. Until that date, courses in the area could be called "bachelor's degree in Computer Science", "Systems Analysis", "bachelor's degree in Informatics", "Computer Engineering", "Computer Engineering", and so on. Generally, there was no correspondence between the name of the course and the type of training that was offered. After the year 2000, the courses in the area were defined by the Commission of Specialists in Teaching Computing and Informatics, of the Ministry of Education, in just five denominations:

- Bachelor in Computer Science.
- Bachelor in Information Systems.
- Degree in Computing.
- Bachelor in Computer Engineering.
- Bachelor in Software Engineering.

Such classification, however, is still imprecise, and in many cases a degree in Informatics can perfectly perform the duties of a degree in Information Systems. On the other hand, a Computer Engineer can teach computer classes, and so on.

If the ideas are already diffused in the nomenclature of the courses, let alone in the research carried out by professionals in the area.

This chapter presents a possible classification for the types of research carried out in Computer Science and related areas, considering the degree of maturity of research in the specific subarea, as well as its interrelationship with other sciences. This classification is based on a discussion that took place on the sbc-l@sbc.org.br list in the 1990s.

Possibly, the area has already matured a lot in recent years, and less and less works of a less mature type are being presented (we have no data on this; this is a conjecture). But even so, this chapter serves as an alert to new researchers, students who are entering their careers, of the difficulties encountered in the past, thus pointing to a better path to be followed.

5.1 Presentation of a Product

Among the emerging areas within Computing, that is, those that even for Computing are considered very new, a research that simply seeks to present something new is acceptable. In these areas, research is eminently exploratory, making it difficult to compare a work with previous ones, as these may not exist or are not yet available in the main search engines. Much emerging literature ends up being initially published as gray literature, that is, documents published as technical reports, drafts or even on web pages and blogs, which are therefore not as easily locatable as indexed publications.

Therefore, research in these areas would present results of the form: "I did something new. Here is my product." It is very unlikely that more mature areas will recognize research presented in this way.

For example: an article of the "new method for teaching programming" type would hardly be accepted in a programming teaching event, unless the author clearly presents the problems with the old methods (control) and how his new method solves them. solve.

Another example consists of articles or works that present a tool or a prototype. If tool development has not been preceded by at least a systematic mapping of existing tools, there will be little or no effectiveness in comparing what has been developed with other tools.

In any case, presentations of this type are usually naive and should be avoided. Even if you are working in a new area of knowledge, it is interesting that research shows that you are solving a relevant problem. If the problem is relevant, it is likely that it has already been tried to solve it, and from there it is possible to draw a comparison. The catapult student, mentioned earlier, came up with a solution to the problem without having been aware of other solutions that existed and, therefore, failed in his research.

One type of article that fits very well into this category is one where the student develops a system and writes an article to present it. There are no comparisons, no new knowledge is presented, other than the system itself and, therefore, this type of article has little chance of being accepted in a relevant publication vehicle. Often, such articles are seen more as propaganda for the group that developed the system than as a scientific contribution. In other words, "tool manual" type articles should be avoided. And for all that is most sacred, may Figure 1 in the article not be the system login screen!

This type of publication may have its space in special sessions for the presentation of tools or in events whose theme is the application of Informatics to some other area, such as Medicine, Education and others. Even so, these areas have increasingly demanded that the articles presented are more than a mere description of a system, that they bring new knowledge to the area and, above all, compare the work presented with previous works.

The development of a system and its presentation can be considered relevant work in undergraduate or specialization courses, as long as it is evident that the student has applied techniques in the system or in the system development process learned during the course. This type of work would hardly be accepted in master's and doctoral degrees, or even in professional master's degrees in which, despite the practical application of the solution, it must be produced from science and not just from technology.

5.2 Presentation of Something Different

A second type of research, a little more mature, consists of presenting a different way of solving a problem. This type of research is also characteristic of emerging areas, and the works are generally presented as a simple comparison between techniques, in which scientific rigor is not necessarily required in the presentation of results. Comparisons are usually much more qualitative than quantitative.

The results of such an article may be accepted in any publication vehicle, provided that the arguments used by the author are convincing. But possibly it will be a borderline article, accepted only in the absence of better ones.

A case study rarely proves anything, and the possibility of generalizing the result is the responsibility of the author of the text, not the reader. If the method worked in evidentiary case study A or case study B, that doesn't mean it will always work. There is, therefore, no proof with scientific rigor, but an attempt to convince the reader.

Despite this, the case study can serve to prove that an established method fails in one or another situation, that is, a theory is refuted. This result could be interesting especially if the reason for the failure was clearly identified and a solution to the problem was proposed and validated.

This type of research is typical in new areas where large databases are not available to test theories empirically or where the time and resources required to carry out the research empirically are unfeasible.

For this type of research to work, it is necessary to have a good working hypothesis, a good theory built to support it, and a good argument to make an eventual reader convinced of the validity of the theory, even without being able to test it. it with statistically accepted methods.

Regarding the hypothesis, it should be mentioned that it is the heart of the monograph. If the hypothesis is poorly chosen, the work may not achieve the objectives. In that case, who is penalized? The student! Therefore, a good hypothesis with evidence of effectiveness should be sought.

Master's and doctoral works, in general, propose something: a new method, a new idea, a new system, etc. However, "proposing" something is easy. It is difficult to show that the proposal presents some kind of improvement in relation to other similar proposals that exist out there.

For example, proposing a more efficient text compression method than those currently on the market is possible and even commendable as a monograph objective. But the problem is: how to create a more efficient method than the current ones? You need to have a good guess.

A hypothesis is a probable but not yet demonstrated theory or an admissible assumption. The hypothesis guides the research work precisely because it is not yet known whether it is actually true. It will be tested throughout the work. If confirmed, the work will have been a success. If not confirmed, it will be necessary to gather the pieces and try another line of research. That is why it is necessary to have a well-grounded and justified hypothesis. The risk is always with the student.

Once the artifacts used to solve the problem in question and the main characteristics of these artifacts have been identified, a new artifact can be created or defined, covering all the characteristics, as shown in Table 5.2.

This new artifact will be different from the others, as none of the other artifacts alone have their set of characteristics. The new artifact will be useful insofar as the characteristics are effectively relevant. The comparative table will be a good research tool if the characteristics can be effectively and independently verified.

There are three key points in this table:

- The artifacts must have been selected after a systematic mapping, not necessarily carried out by the author of the work, and indicate which are the most relevant based on some objective criterion, such as, for example, being cited in at least two different articles.
- The characteristics must be relevant, that is, they must be important from the identification of possible difficulties with the current tools. For example, a study that compared tools for building sprint backlogs cited as important characteristics whether cells could be expanded, whether the tool allowed shared editing, access across multiple platforms, etc. Features irrelevant in practice should not be included.
- The assessment of whether or not each artifact has the characteristic must be objective and truthful. If the researcher is in doubt or cannot find information about whether a particular artifact has a feature, it is better to say so explicitly than to guess.

This type of research is usually classified as qualitative research, in which one seeks to assess the existence or not of certain properties. But many research papers can benefit from more quantitative data analysis. This brings us to the next type.

Table 5.1 Example of a comparative table of artifacts and characteristics

	feature 1	feature 2	feature 3	feature 4

Artifact 1	X	X		
Artifact 2	X			X
Artifact 3		X	X	X

Table 5.2 Proposal of a new artifact that has all the characteristics of the previous ones

	feature 1	feature 2	feature 3	feature 4
Artifact 1	X	X		
Artifact 2	X			X
Artifact 3		X	X	X
new artifact	X	X	X	X

5.3 Presenting Something Presumably Better

Areas that are a little more mature than the previous ones require that any new approach presented be quantitatively compared with others in the literature. In the absence of internationally accepted or accessible databases (benchmarks), the author of the article ends up creating and carrying out tests that demonstrate that his approach is better than others.

One problem with this type of research is that the author will have to test his approach as well as others in the literature, resulting in overwork, as well as possibly introducing the risk of bias, as there is no guarantee that the approaches presented in the literature have been tested under the best conditions by the author of the work. Therefore, such comparisons are often foolhardy. For a research of this type to be well accepted, it is necessary for the author to make it very clear how he applied each of the techniques and to isolate all the factors that could possibly affect the results.

In any case, an approach to a given problem that proves to be better than other approaches requires some care. First, the researcher must make sure that he is comparing the new approach with one that is state-of-the-art. In computing, it is often inadmissible to present a method and compare it with another one from a bibliographic reference from 20 years ago. Even if the new method is better than the old one, the article will have little credibility unless the author makes it very clear that in the last 20 years there has been no advance in this area. An article, however, that presents improvements over a recently published process, say, a year or two at the most, will have more relevance.

It is not necessary, however, for the author of some new method to demonstrate that his method is better than another state-of-the-art method for every situation. It is often possible to present methods or approaches that work best in certain situations. In this case, the article should make it very clear in which situations the new approach works best and why. Experiments should be done to demonstrate such an improvement.

5.4 Introducing Something Admittedly Better

The most mature level of research in this line, in which the presentation of empirical data is relevant for the acceptance of the results, is the one in which a work is developed and its results are presented according to standardized and internationally accepted tests. In this case, the author of the work does not need to test other approaches, as their results are already published. The author should fetch the input data to test his approach against a known database and present the results using a community-accepted metric. In this way, the experiments can be reproduced by independent teams. If the new approach is shown to be superior to previous approaches, it will be considered state of the art.

Research that presents results of this type is typical of good doctoral theses. It is assumed that, after the publication of the results, no one will be able to ignore this new approach due to the advantages it offers in relation to the previous ones. This is what is meant by "advancing the state of the art".

Amazingly, this is the easiest research to perform, as long as the author has a good working hypothesis. Why that? Because the standard tests are already defined and the data is already available. Just implement the approach and run the tests. The big problem and the inherent difficulty, then, is finding a good working hypothesis that makes sense and is promising (this, unfortunately, is often not trivial).

Therefore, this type of research will require, on the part of the author, a broad study of the state of the art in a given area and a lot of reflection on the way techniques are developed to solve the problems in this area. Open problems will be excellent focuses of attention for research.

In addition, it can be of great value if the author has knowledge in other areas, which are often not even related to the problem in question. Sometimes, techniques from different areas applied to a problem produce very interesting results. However, it must be remembered that just applying a different technique to a problem sends the work to "presenting something different". When choosing to use an alien technique on a known problem, it is necessary to have good reason to believe that the technique can produce better results than current techniques.

The different types of research presented above fall into the sub-areas of Computing in which results are usually presented from empirical evidence or at least from arguments or case studies that suggest proofs of concept.

Another type of research requires formal proofs, according to the rules of logic. The area of formal methods or compilers, for example, will hardly accept works that do not present formal proofs of correctness or efficiency.

A theory must be built, clearly stating which concepts are used and showing that the application of these concepts logically leads to certain results. These results can be the demonstration that a certain algorithm is the best possible algorithm to solve a certain type of problem or that an algorithm to solve a certain type of problem does not exist, or even that the complexity of any algorithm that solves a certain type of problem cannot be smaller than a given polynomial.

5.6 Discussion

From the observations made, it can be seen that different subareas of Computing can be characterized by different styles of research. You can classify these styles, then, into three basic types:

- *Formal surveys*, where the elaboration of a theory and a formal proof that the theory is correct is required. Formal logic will be the great work tool of the researcher who opts for this line.
- *empirical research*, in which a new approach is compared with others through community-accepted tests. Statistical methods will be the great work tool of the researcher who opts for this line. Those interested in carrying out this type of research should deepen their knowledge of Applied Statistics and for this a good reference is Barbetta (2007).
- *exploratory research*, in which it is not possible to prove a theory or present statistically accepted results. This is where case studies, qualitative analyzes and exploratory research in emerging areas come in. Argumentation and persuasion are the main tools of the researcher.

Although formal research is apparently more difficult to carry out, its results, when obtained, are more difficult to refute.

Empirical research, even based on statistical methods, can be refutable if it is not also based on good theory, because statistics do not explain causes. The anecdote of the researcher who ordered a spider to jump and then tore off one of its legs is well known. After ripping off seven legs, the spider still jumped with its remaining leg. After ripping off the last leg, the scientist realized that the spider was no longer responding to the order to jump. The researcher's conclusion was that the spider without legs is deaf, as he no longer heard the order to jump. Could this theory withstand Occam's blade?

Lastly, exploratory research seems to be easier to carry out, because it is not necessary to use the methods of formal logic or to carry out exhaustive experiments. However, in terms of research, it is the riskiest approach, as the acceptance of arguments is not universal, and articles that are not based on a good theory and/or a good set of tests are less likely to be published in good vehicles.. The presentation of case studies and examples, in the case of exploratory research, may help the researcher to convince the reader of his point of view, but they do not constitute evidence.

Research Elements

Preparing a research paper is a step that must be carried out before writing about research begins. It sounds strange, but this is often a point that should be stressed. Students, eager to write the monograph, start writing pages and pages without having done any research.

Therefore, it is not recommended that the student start writing his monograph without having carried out some research that has produced new knowledge. To put it better: there is no need to start writing the bibliographic review chapter before knowing what will actually be done in terms of knowledge production.

The literature review of a research paper in Computing, in general, should not be a treaty about the research area. Often, a student who starts writing the review chapter before deciding on the research objective will end up writing too much and unnecessarily. This chapter will be tiring for the reader and, many times, he will not understand why certain subjects are placed there if they are not covered in the monograph itself.

This chapter presents several suggestions that can help a novice researcher design his or her scientific research project. In particular, the sections considered mandatory in research works will be commented, which include the choice of one or more objectives, hypotheses, justifications, results and limitations of a work.

6.1 Objectives

The secret to successful research work is to have a good objective. Once the objective of the work is defined, everything else revolves around it. The rationale will tell you why this goal is worth pursuing; the methodological procedure informs how the objective can be achieved; the expected results show what changes in the world after the objective is reached; the bibliographic review will present the concepts necessary for understanding the objective and other works that sought the same objective.

Not every goal can be considered a good research objective. For example, something like "the objective of this work is to increase my knowledge in the area of study" (actual case), may even be very sincere, but it does not convince anyone that some new knowledge for Humanity will be produced. So this must be avoided.

Another objective, sometimes found, is the form "propose...". Something is proposed, usually a method, an approach, a technique, an algorithm, a comparison, or whatever. The question is, if the author makes the proposal, will the objective be achieved? If the student proposes to propose and has proposed, then he is proposed! What is proposed is not necessarily better or different from what has gone before. So, the research stage in this case is still one of the most naive. It is necessary that the objective says that what is being proposed is better than what already exists, or that this solves a problem that could not be solved before.

According to Carleton professor John W. Chinneck, the description of a research problem has three parts:[1]

1. A precise statement of the question or problem addressed in the monograph.

2. An explanation by direct reference to the bibliography that such a research question has not yet been addressed.

3. A discussion of why it is important to address this research question.

   Item 2 will fail if the student cannot make it clear that the research question has never been addressed. A good literature review is necessary to present such justification with sufficient authority. Statements such as "I have not found anything similar" should be avoided. The student should always show what he has found in the relevant sources he has examined and compare what he has found with what he intends to do. If he says he didn't find anything, the examining board will likely think he hasn't done his research properly or is dealing with a problem of little interest. In some cases, it may happen that actually nothing very similar is found, but in any case there is always some problem that can be considered as close as possible. There will be situations where almost identical approaches will be found, varying in few details; in other cases, the closest approach will be so distinct that a good deal of explanation will be needed to understand why it is relevant. Leonardo da Vinci did not know the technology used by modern airplanes and probably did not find much bibliography on the subject, so he based his studies on flying machines on the closest model that was available at the time: the flight structure of birds.

   Despite this, ancient knowledge should not be completely ignored. Often, ancient knowledge combined with the state of the art can produce very interesting results. In the case of the aeronautical industry, for example, attempts are now made to produce flexible airplanes that, in a certain way, imitate the flight structures of birds. But this is done on the basis of current knowledge; we are not reinventing the wheel, but improving existing concepts.

6.1.1 Path to Choosing a Research Objective

In order for someone to be able to think of a relevant research objective, they must know the area of research in which they are working. Therefore, the logical path consists of three steps:

1. *Choose a research topic*, that is, an area of knowledge in which to work.
2. *Perform the bibliographic review*. Unless the author is already an expert in the chosen field, he will need to read many works already published in this field to know what is being done (state of the art) and what still needs to be done (open problems).
3. *Define the research objective*. Once the literature review is done, the research objective will possibly be strongly related to one of the open problems verified in the previous step.

It is still possible that steps 2 and 3 must be repeated a few times in order to refine the objective. In fact, when carrying out a literature review on a given topic, the researcher will have ideas about aspects of the topic that have not yet been explored, and these aspects may give rise to a research objective. But, before starting to spend energy trying to achieve this objective, the researcher must refine his bibliographic research trying to verify if this objective has not already been pursued in previous works and what kind of result was obtained.

In the history of the catapult, the research topic was the river that ran through the city. When the research objective "finding a safe way to cross the river" was established, the student should have checked the literature for the main works already published on river crossings. But he limited himself only to information about the composition of rivers and, therefore, he missed very important information for his research, namely, that methods for crossing rivers already existed and that he should first try to improve these already existing methods or at least get to know them. and its flaws, before embarking on the search for something totally new. At the extreme of this reasoning is the possibility that a few years earlier other researchers had already tried to use the catapult to cross rivers, without knowing each other. Each time the study is repeated,

6.1.2 Theme

The research topic often depends on the interest of the student and advisor. It is not recommended that a research be carried out whose theme is not compatible with the supervisor's knowledge. In the case of the student, it is recommended that, when going from undergraduate to master's and from master's to doctorate, try to work on the same topic, although seeking different goals. Why that? Because, if the student stays on the topic, the bibliographic review step will be completed more quickly when moving from one stage to another in their training. It will be enough for him to keep up to date with the latest developments in the area to be able to decide on a good research objective. If the student changes topic, he will have to do the entire bibliographic review on another topic, which will take a lot of time.

It is not impossible for a person with training in one area to obtain a master's or doctorate degree in a different area, but he will have more work and it will take more time to mature the concepts of the new area than a person who already has experience in the area.

The theme can be specialized from a large area into increasingly specific sub-areas. For example:

1. Computer Science.
1.1 Artificial intelligence.
1.1.1 Search methods.
1.1.1.1 Heuristic search.
1.1.1.1.1 Algorithm A*.

In this list, each item is a specialization of the previous item, but each is just a research topic, albeit increasingly specific.

Going in the other direction, one can combine a research topic with an application area. The topic, possibly, will be more specific than general. It does not make much sense, for example, to speak of "application of algorithms to the problem of paving roads". A research topic such as "application of heuristic search to the problem of transporting road paving machines" would make more sense.

Even so, in some cases there are works whose theme is something like "application of artificial intelligence techniques to solve problem X". The researcher must have the notion of proportion to know if the level of specificity of the research topic is adequate or not. In the previous example, when talking about artificial intelligence, a huge range of possibilities opens up (it can be seen how extensive the area is in Russell and Norvig [2004]). Therefore, a topic as extensive as this is not adequate. When talking about heuristic search, however, the range is reduced to relatively few known algorithms, and the topic becomes more viable. The broader the topic, the greater the number of books and articles that will have to be read. Therefore, it is recommended to seek increasingly specific topics before proposing a research objective. When choosing a research topic that has application in another area, care must be taken. When doing a Masters or Doctorate in Computer Science, it should be noted that the main contribution of the work must be to the area of Computing.

6.1.3 Research Problem

A monograph must present a solution to a problem. Initially, therefore, a problem must be identified. It would be wrong to start the monograph simply by deciding to create a new method for this or that. A new method should only be created if it solves a problem that the old methods don't solve.

In the case of the catapult, the student proposed and tested a new method for crossing rivers. Here comes an interesting question. According to the student, the problem was to cross the river. But this identified problem is no longer an unsolved problem because there are different approaches to crossing a river: bridge, ferry, cable car, etc. So, if the student wanted to insist on this theme, he would have to indicate which problems the existing solutions present. That is, what are the problems encountered when trying to cross a river with a bridge or a ferry? He could find, for example, that bridges are too expensive and ferries are too slow. If all existing solutions present some kind of problem, it is possible that a new approach is being paved the way. Otherwise,

Some research proposals are initially presented without having a clearly identified problem. For example: "This paper proposes to use the anthill metaphor to model packets in a network." This topic may even turn out to be an interesting work, but what problem will this modeling solve? What is wrong with other forms of modeling, whatever they may be, that this anthill metaphor is likely to solve?

If the author cannot clearly establish the problem addressed in his monograph, it will be very difficult for other people to speculate on the possible uses of it. It will also be difficult to assess whether she was successful.

6.1.4 Professional Perspective

The research topic to be chosen, at any level of training, in addition to being to the student's liking, must be related to his/her professional development perspective.

It doesn't make sense to spend several years investing in research in area X and then work the rest of your life in area Y. Ideally, each research would generate innovation, that is, some kind of product or an improvement to an existing product that could, after the end of the course, generate some perspective of work and income for the researcher and benefits for society.

6.1.5 Formulation of the Objective

The research objective must be directly verifiable at the end of the work. A good research objective will possibly demonstrate that some hypothesis being tested is or is not true.

Therefore, the general objective and the specific objectives of the work must be expressed in the form of a non-trivial condition whose success can be verified at the end of the work. A well-expressed objective will generally have verbs like "demonstrate", "prove", "improve" (according to some defined metric), etc.

Care must be taken with certain verbs that determine goals whose verification is trivial and therefore inappropriate. Among them we can mention "propose", "study", "present", etc. If the objective of the work is to propose something, it is enough for the thing to be proposed for the objective to be achieved and, therefore, this form is trivial and inadequate, since the definition of the objective does not mention the quality of what will be proposed.

If the objective of the work is to study something, it will have been achieved if it has been studied, regardless of whether any new information has been learned or not, and is therefore inappropriate as a research objective. Studying is usually the student's goal and not the job.

If the purpose of the work is to present something, again it is trivial and inappropriate. A simple presentation does not necessarily produce new knowledge. For example, "the objective of this work is to present the operators of Boolean logic"; such an objective can be achieved with a short text explaining the known operators, but, as it does not bring new information, it is not a research objective, it is a class.

The proposal, study and presentation can be justifiable as a research objective as long as the object of the proposal, study or presentation is something original.

According to Chinneck, a monograph must present an original contribution to knowledge. In this way, at the end of the work, the student should be able to show that he identified a problem that was worth solving, but that had not yet been solved. In addition, the student must show that he has solved the problem he proposed and present the solution.

As a result, Chinneck concludes that an evaluator, when reading the text of a monograph, will seek to answer the following questions:

- What is the research question that the student proposed?
- Is it a good question? (Has it ever been answered? Is it worth answering?)
- Was the student able to convince that the question was answered properly?
- Did the student make an adequate contribution to knowledge?

Another issue is that sometimes the student confuses the research objective with the means to obtain this objective. A student, for example, concerned about the efficiency of text compression algorithms, might set the goal of "defining a new model of neural networks to perform text compression". But this is not the student's actual goal. His goal is to define a more efficient compression model than the existing ones. Implementing the neural network is a means to achieve this, but it is not the goal itself. Therefore, great care must be taken in formulating the objective.

6.1.6 Extension of Purpose

A research objective, depending on the desired education level (undergraduate, specialization, master's or doctorate), cannot be too trivial or too complex.

An objective that is too trivial will be achieved quickly, but it will hardly be defensible before a panel, because with each academic degree, the student is expected not only to be inspired, but also to perspire, that is, it is not enough to have a good idea, it is necessary to work on it. it demonstrating all its different aspects within the level of complexity required by the desired degree.

A very complex objective will hardly be achieved in the time available to fulfill the requirements of the desired degree. Complex goals can be placed as long-term projects in the career of researchers who have already graduated, who will often have decades ahead and research teams to pursue these goals.

Undergraduate and graduate students must achieve the objectives set within the regulatory time that their courses set and therefore the complexity of these objectives must be consistent with that time. It is not enough for a degree to present a complex idea that cannot be demonstrated or completed in the time available. Claiming to the bank that there was no time to complete the work is hardly a good excuse.

Therefore, the student should always seek support from the advisor and the definition of a research objective that can be met in the available time, according to the course taken. The more experienced the advisor, that is, the more jobs he has successfully guided in his life, the more he can be expected to be able to support the student in choosing an appropriate goal.

6.1.7 Research Objective versus Technical Objective

It is acceptable that an undergraduate and even a specialization work has technical objectives, that is, it is expected in these degrees that students are able to demonstrate that they have learned certain concepts and are able to put them into practice. Thus, it is acceptable for an undergraduate student, at the end of their course, to develop a system using concepts learned during the course and to present the system as a final work. However, this type of approach is not acceptable at the master's and doctoral levels. It is expected that the master and the doctor have somehow contributed to the advancement of knowledge. Thus, the development of a system, although it may be necessary to prove some previously established hypothesis, is not in itself sufficient for the granting of a master's or doctoral degree.

If the simple development of a system or a prototype were enough to grant an academic degree, universities should be granting a master's degree to all programmers or analysts who daily develop systems, often complex, in their companies. If this does not happen, it is because there is something else in the dissertations and theses that needs to be looked for. That something else is scientific knowledge. A monograph is a document that presents, in an organized way, a contribution to the state of the art, presenting, therefore, information that was not known and that, from the moment they are published, become part of the relevant body of knowledge for those who work in certain area.

Technical jobs that are acceptable at undergraduate and major only use knowledge already available. Scientific works, which must be developed in the master's and doctorate, must, in addition to using the knowledge already available, create knowledge, associating them within a coherent structure with those that are already known. Therefore, the development of systems or prototypes will only serve as support to demonstrate the applicability of this new knowledge, if necessary.

6.1.8 Specific Objectives

The specific objectives must be chosen in the same way as the general objective, that is, they must be non-trivial and verifiable at the end of the work. Typically, specific objectives are not work steps, but by-products. Care must be taken not to confuse the specific objectives with the steps of the methodological procedure. Thus, specific objectives such as carrying out a literature review, choosing an approach, defining a prototype, executing an experiment, etc. should be avoided as they are intermediate steps. The specific objective should indicate a contribution to knowledge, such as a hypothesis to be demonstrated, a theory to be refined or refuted, etc.

It should be understood, therefore, that the specific objectives are details or by-products of the general objective. If the general objective is to prove a certain hypothesis, the specific objectives can establish the proof of a series of conditions associated with that hypothesis.

For example, in the case of the student who wants to better understand self-managed teams, one might imagine that their overall objective would be to see if self-managed teams work better than manager-based teams. Specific objectives could be a breakdown of what "better" means in this context. For example, he could set as specific objectives to verify if self-managed teams are more productive, if their members feel happier, if their products are better, according to some defined metrics, etc. All these different dimensions of analysis constitute the meaning of "best" of the overall objective.

6.2 Methodological Procedure

In general, monographs have a chapter or section labeled "methodology". However, methodology would be the study of methods. Despite the current usage, from the point of view of language, it would be more correct to say that an individual scientific work has a methodological procedure and not a methodology.

It is difficult for a student who is writing a monograph to present a methodology, unless he compares different methodological approaches and, as a result, selects the best one. But the usual thing is that, depending on the type of problem, a pure or mixed methodological procedure is chosen and that it is followed until the hypothesis is proved or refuted.

The most appropriate methodological procedure for a scientific work can normally only be established after the research objective has been identified.

The methodological procedure consists of the sequence of steps necessary to demonstrate that the proposed objective has been achieved, that is, if the steps defined in the procedure are performed correctly, the results obtained must be convincing.

The methodological procedure should then indicate whether a systematic review will be carried out, whether interviews will be carried out, prototypes will be developed, whether theoretical models will be built, whether experiments will be carried out, how the data will be organized and compared, and so on, depending on the objective. from work.

The definition of the methodological procedure, or method, is a fundamental step to be performed immediately after defining the objective. Given the objective, the methodological procedure describes the way to reach it. Thus, it should be enough to follow the path described by the methodological procedure to reach the objective. If the objective and the methodological procedure are coherent, a difficult part of the research work will have already been carried out, leaving only the execution of the steps described in the methodological procedure.

However, describing a set of steps that constitute an acceptable methodological procedure requires some knowledge about the scientific method that was detailed in Chapter 3. Failure to observe the scientific method can lead to wrong or forced conclusions.

Methodologically naive proposals are not at all uncommon in computing. Things like "working with two groups, one with the tool and one without the tool (control)" could even be part of a methodological procedure, but it is not enough. If the difference between the means of the two groups is 0.5 percentage point, can it be concluded that one group was better than the other? Or could it have been by chance? What if the difference is five percentage points? How to know? There are some information brought by statistics that should be known to anyone who ventures to develop scientific research.

In addition, there is still the possibility of misuse of logic. The ancient Sophists were much in demand among the Greeks for argumentation. However, the logic used by them was not always exactly what could be accepted from a scientific point of view. A hilarious example of the devious use of logic appears in the movie Monty Python's Search for the Holy Grail, when Bedevere proposes a foolproof method for determining a witch's identity. At the end of a series of pseudological arguments, he concludes that if a woman weighs as much as a duck, she is a witch. Basically, according to Bedevere, witches burn and wood also burns. Wood floats on water, just like ducks. So if the woman weighs as much as a duck, she is made of wood and therefore is a witch.

Furthermore, it is important that the methodological procedure is more than a simple list of steps. For example, if the student defines his procedure as "review literature; define requirements; implement prototype; evaluate prototype", it will be necessary to detail more how this evaluation will be carried out. Would it be a case study of evidence? Was it by controlled experimentation? Would it be by surveying expert opinion? So it is not enough to say what will be done in the work, it is necessary to show that what will be done will lead with some certainty to some conclusion.

Ideally, in the case of empirical research, it is necessary to detail how the samples will be collected, how they will be analyzed, and how the results will be judged by statistical tests.

6.2.1 Data versus Concepts

The research method is not just about collecting data to support the working hypothesis. It is necessary to elaborate a thoughtful and enlightening speech from these data. The most important aspect of a monograph is critical thinking and not just gathering information. Academic works that are restricted to conducting opinion polls through questionnaires with the consequent tabulation of data and presentation of graphs will not be valid if they do not bring some new information. And new information will only appear in a descriptive analysis of these data or in the formulation of theories that seek to explain cause and effect (for example, why do the data behave in such a way?).

Lakatos and Marconi (2006) identify the questionnaire as a research instrument that does not require the presence of the researcher. However, you should avoid distributing questionnaires to be answered if you do not know in advance what information you are looking for, that is, what hypothesis you are trying to prove. Even in cases of exploratory research, there must be some hypothesis or intuition on the part of the researcher regarding the existence of some sufficiently important phenomenon that deserves to be studied.

Also, in general, straight answers and simplistic interpretations are not the most interesting. For example, some time ago researchers conducted a survey in England, where they interviewed men and women asking how many sexual partners they had had in their lifetime. The average score for women was 3, and the average score for men was 10. A naive and simplistic interpretation of this fact would say that men, on average, have more partners than women. However, considering that there are approximately the same number of men and women in society, this is impossible, since every time a man has a new partner, a woman (the partner) also automatically has a new partner. Therefore, the two averages should be practically the same. The conclusion of the research was, therefore, that men lie more or women lie less, or both lie when it comes to quantifying the number of partners. Thus, in the case of survey research application, the ideal is to seek to discover more than the obvious.

One should also do everything possible to avoid bias. The ideal in a survey is that the sample of respondents is chosen at random and that everyone responds. Questionnaires sent to 1000 people that are answered by only 30 are likely to be biased. Imagine if the question were "do you usually answer questionnaires sent by email?".

6.2.2 Constitutive and Operational Definitions

In a monograph, the researcher will often need to define terms they are using. There are two basic ways to create definitions: constitutive and operational definitions. Depending on the type of term, you will need to use one or the other.

Eminently formal works tend to use constitutive definitions more. According to Kerlinger (1980), "constitutive definitions are dictionary definitions". Constitutive definitions seek to define a term in terms of its constituents. A formal grammar, for example, can be defined as a set of production rules; a production rule can be defined as two sequences of symbols, and so on.

However, research that uses less formal terms such as "ease", "adequacy", "flexibility", etc. they will hardly be able to use only constitutive definitions for these terms.

In these cases, it is necessary to use an operational definition that, according to Kerlinger (1980): "Assigns meaning to a construct or variable by specifying the activities or 'operations' necessary to measure or manipulate it." The operational definition is, then, a pragmatic definition. It does not define the nature of a phenomenon, but the means to obtain a measurement, and characterizes the result of that measurement as being the phenomenon itself.

For example, the term "ease" can be defined as the number of strokes on the keyboard or mouse to perform a certain task. The term "adequacy" can be defined as the score obtained in a standard test applied by experts. The term "flexibility" can be defined as the average time it takes a programmer to introduce a predefined set of features.

The important thing here is to emphasize that, in the case of terms that represent non-formal characteristics, it is necessary to use operational definitions so that the phenomenon associated with the term can be effectively measured. Without this, the work would only be speculative.

6.2.3 Variables

The existence of phenomena for which the scientist is interested in carrying out objective measurements was mentioned earlier. In general, such phenomena that can be objectively measured are identified as variables. A variable is a name given to a phenomenon that can be measured and that varies according to the measurement. If it did not vary, it would be a constant and would not be of greater interest to the research.

Variables in experiments, like variables in computer programs, have a domain, that is, a set of values within which the variable changes. For example, a temperature in general will be a rational number limited from below by absolute zero (the literal value will depend on the scale used). A variable related to temperature cannot assume the value "XYZ" or false, as these do not belong to the numerical domain.

The domain of a variable can be discrete or continuous. Continuous variables take on real values; the idea of continuum comes from the fact that between two values there is always a third. On the other hand, discrete variables assume their values in sets whose elements can be ordered or in finite sets. The number of participants in a videoconference is a phenomenon represented in a variable whose domain is discrete and corresponds to the set of natural numbers. The values of this set can be ordered, and between the nth value and the (n+1)th value there is no third possibility for any n that is a natural number.

Some discrete variables take on their values in finite sets. Such variables are called categorical. For example, the grades that a student can obtain in a subject can be defined in the set {A, B, C, D, E}. The existence of a certain characteristic in an artifact can be classified in the set {exists, does not exist, partially exists, does not apply}.

In science, observed phenomena are often classified with categorical variables, as they are generally easier to understand than continuous values. If students with continuous values were evaluated, would it be reasonable to conclude that a student with a grade of 6.7812 is better than a student with a grade of 6.7811?

In some cases, it is possible to establish rules for transforming continuous to discrete values. This process, called discretization, consists of assigning a different discrete value to various intervals of continuous values. For example, considering grades rounded to one decimal place after the comma, a correspondence between the continuous domain and the categorical variable can be established as follows: grades from 0.0 to 4.9 could be considered grade E; grades from 5.0 to 5.9, grade D; grades from 6.0 to 6.9, grade C; grades from 7.0 to 8.9, grade B, and grades from 9.0 to 10.0, grade A. Note, however, that when rounding to one decimal place after the decimal point is applied, the domain of the variable has already been transformed from continuous to discrete because, in this way, the possible scores are limited to 101 values:

In experimental research, it is also important to classify the variables as measured or manipulated. A measured variable is one whose phenomenon will be observed by the researcher. For example, how many times a user of a tool will look in the manual for information to perform the task that was proposed to him. This variable has as its domain the set of natural numbers, and its values are not determined by the observer, but simply measured.

The manipulated variable is the one that the experimenter will deliberately modify to carry out his experiment. For this reason, such a variable is also called an experimental variable. An example of a manipulated variable could be the number of steps of the task passed on to users. The researcher could give some users, for example, tasks with five steps; to others, with ten steps; to others, with fifteen steps, etc. Thus, when experimenting, the researcher manipulates the variable referring to the number of steps of the task and observes the behavior of the measured variable, which consists of counting how many times the user will look at the tool manual.

But why do researchers manipulate one or more variables while looking at others? It's because they want to find dependencies between these variables. In the previous example, possibly the researcher would be trying to find out whether or not longer tasks imply that the user consults the system manual more often.

In principle, one can test the dependence between any manipulated and observed variables, but this test will not always make sense. Before analyzing a dependency experimentally, the researcher usually develops a theory or hypothesis. In the previous case, the hypothesis could be that, the larger the task, the greater the consultation of the manual made by the user. Another possible hypothesis would be that no matter the size of the task, it will not influence the number of times the user consults the manual. It's a dependency that, in either case, seems to be worth testing.

But the dependencies that can be tested do not always make sense as a hypothesis or theory. For example, manipulating the variable "number of buttons on the app screen" and measuring the variable "number of times the user sneezes while using the tool" can be fun, but there is hardly a connection between the two phenomena. Another example would be looking at the day of the week and trying to see if programs run faster on Friday. The researcher could even create controlled experiments to measure this, but he would hardly find a connection between the day of the week and the speed of the programs. Also because current theory about programs does not establish any connection between their speed and the day of the week. Such a hypothesis would then prove to be flawed.

Hence the importance of working with a good hypothesis in research. It is not enough to carry out experiments and find relationships between variables. It is necessary to have a theory that tries to explain the reason for these relationships.

An experimental research hypothesis, then, will generally have an implication, that is, antecedent/consequent, association between one or more independent variables and one or more dependent variables. For example, does the number of steps in a task increase the number of times the user consults the manual? This would be a research hypothesis in which the dependent variable is the number of consultations to the manual, and the independent variable is the number of steps in the task. In general, the researcher manipulates the independent variable and measures the dependent one. In this case, as both variables are numerical, it can be said that a direct correlation is sought, that is, the greater the number of steps, the greater the number of queries. In other cases, one could search for inverse correlations,

There is still linear and non-linear dependence. Linear dependence can be approximated by a first degree polynomial. For example, it could be observed that for each step in the task, the user makes two more queries to the manual. In this case, the relationship between the number of steps x and the number of queries y could be expressed by the function $y = 2x$.

*Nonlinear Dependencies*they are usually represented by polynomials of degree greater than one or by equations with exponentials, roots or logarithms. For the reader who wants to delve into other forms of dependence, it is recommended to read a good book on Statistics, such as the one by Barbetta, Reis and Bornia (2008).

6.3 Research Hypothesis

One aspect that differentiates scientific work from technical work is the existence of a research hypothesis. A hypothesis is a statement of which it is not known at first whether it is true or false. The research work consists precisely in trying to prove the truth or falsity of the hypothesis.

A goal without a good hypothesis can be very risky. Earlier it was said that the objective is to try to produce some knowledge that does not yet exist. But if there is not a good hypothesis to justify this objective, there is a risk of carrying out the research without obtaining results. For example, having as a research objective to prove that P = NP is perfectly valid, as this problem is relevant to society, and the knowledge needed to solve the problem does not yet exist. However, with which hypothesis will the researcher work? If the research problem is simply stated as "prove that P = NP", the researcher may be left groping, and the risk of failure will be very great. It is therefore necessary to have a hypothesis.

A thesis consists of a hypothesis or conjecture. The thesis text or monograph is a document in which the student presents arguments in favor of his thesis. Hence the confusion that is often made with the term "thesis", which can represent both the written document and the research hypothesis.

The methodological procedure, as discussed above, should indicate how the tests are to be carried out. At the end of the experiments there will be evidence for or against the initial hypothesis. In that case, one might ask, "What if you can't prove that the hypothesis was valid?" The answer to this question will depend on how relevant the original hypothesis was. Any hypothesis chosen at random, without any kind of justification, if not confirmed, does not bring any new information to the research area. But a solid and well-justified hypothesis with evidence of validity, which is ultimately invalidated, can still yield interesting information. In the worst case, it will prove that what could eventually be intuitively accepted as true has not stood the test. This is how many myths can be debunked.

Therefore, in addition to the objective, hypothesis and methodological procedure, it is essential that the research work is based on a good justification for the choice of the hypothesis. A well-justified hypothesis at the beginning of the work increases the chances of success. First, it is more likely to be true than an unwarranted ad hoc hypothesis. Second, if it is false, the work will have the merit of having debunked some common-sense myth.

Scientific work in the field of Computing then consists of formulating a hypothesis and collecting evidence to prove its validity.

A research problem, in general, will ask how two or more variables are related and whether there is a positive or negative correlation between the values of the variables. The existence of these correlations, however, still does not explain causes. A consistent theory that explains cause and effect needs to be developed. This happens because, sometimes, two variables even correlate with a high index, but the causes involved may not be so direct.

An example is the case of a company that decided to check whether well-fed employees worked better. The company started serving a healthy breakfast to its employees in all branches and, in practically all of them, productivity increased. What's the explanation? Well-fed workers work better than poorly-fed workers? It seems to make sense.

But is it really true? Was it really the food that made employees work harder? To verify this, the company tested removing the healthy breakfast to see if workers returned to their former pace. To everyone's surprise, productivity grew even more.

How would a scientist deal with such seemingly contradictory data? The point is that it is a question of verifying the real reason for the increase in productivity. And this was not because of a better diet. A new theory was formulated, explaining that the increase in productivity was due to the feeling of changes in the company. Employees are used to realizing that changes in the company often lead to layoffs. Therefore, every time there is a change in the environment (introduction or withdrawal of breakfast), employees tend to work harder to be noticed and to secure their jobs.

It was commented earlier that a working hypothesis is very risky if it is not solidly supported by a good justification that presents evidence that it is worth investing time and resources in trying to prove the hypothesis. Who in their right mind would propose to work two years to prove that it's better to hire programmers who support a certain football team because they are more productive? A good hypothesis needs to be justifiable, that is, consistent with knowledge of how the world works.

In a monograph, the choice of the research problem must be justified; this is usual. But even more important is to justify the choice of the research hypothesis. For example, if the search topic is "text compression", the search objective is to obtain an algorithm with a higher degree of compression than commercial algorithms. The justification of the research problem could be that the algorithms that compress better are very slow compared to others that compress less. The research objective could then be to define an algorithm that compresses as much as those that compress more, but is as fast as the fastest.

In this case, what is the research hypothesis? The student could, for example, believe that a particular neural network model could be modified to be fast and very compact. But why does he believe this? Read about it somewhere? Have you carried out experiments and observed promising results? Have you reflected on the structure of the network and speculated that you could modify it to achieve your goals?

Choosing the research hypothesis is a bet that is made to solve the research problem. The more evidence the researcher has that this hypothesis is a good bet, the less risk he takes. Thus, the justification of the hypothesis should focus on presenting evidence that the chosen neural network model can produce the expected solution to the research problem.

Sometimes, it is not possible to fully solve the research problem. For example, the algorithm could be almost as fast as the fastest and almost as effective as the most effective. The objective of obtaining a better algorithm in both cases was not achieved. But, maybe this algorithm is still very good, as it gets better and faster results than most others. Another situation that could be reached is the observation that this algorithm is the best only if the text to be compared is written in a certain language. A possible explanation for this could be the fact that the language in question uses or does not use accentuation or has more or less consonants, or even the language's own writing structures. In this case, although the algorithm is not an ideal solution for the general case,

To justify the research hypothesis, it will be necessary to present some evidence that adopting it can lead to good results. These evidences can be references to other works that, eventually, showed some kind of correlated result that points to the viability of the chosen hypothesis or, still, constitute data preliminarily collected by the author of the work himself or in an exploratory case study.

In general, expected results are situations that the author of a work expects to occur if its objectives are achieved. Contrary to objectives, expected results are usually not obtained during the work. They are later. The objectives will be pursued by the author and, at the end of the work, he will say whether or not they were achieved. The expected results will possibly occur after the work becomes known and starts to be adopted by the researchers or professionals affected.

For example, the objective of the work may be to define an effort estimation method for software development that is more accurate than the state-of-the-art methods. The research author should have a good hypothesis to support this objective in the first place. He should carry out a bibliographic research to know the state of the art. Then he could perform a set of experiments that may or may not demonstrate the validity of the hypothesis. The objective of the work would be to obtain a more accurate method than the existing ones. What would be the expected results of this work?

This researcher could initially present, as expected results of his work, the adoption of his method by the industry and the best performance of software producing companies that come to use this estimation method.

As can be seen here, it is practically impossible for the author to obtain these expected results while carrying out his research. But they may eventually occur later. It is also possible that they do not occur because, for any other reason, it may happen that no company adopts their method.

Thus, it can be said that the objectives must be verifiable at the end of the work, including the specific objectives. The expected results are just hopes and cannot necessarily be verified at the end of the work.

At the beginning of the research work, one way of trying to determine what the expected results of the work are is to ask the question: "What would possibly change in the world/industry/society/academy if I achieved the objectives of my research?"

6.6 Work Limitations

Contrary to what beginning students often think, it is not possible to solve all of humanity's problems in two or three years of work. Wanting to do this can be associated with "wanting to change the world syndrome" or "Nobel Prize syndrome" (Mullins and Killey, 2002).

A research work can often start with an objective that is too ambitious and, therefore, unattainable during the time available for the course. Therefore, it is often necessary to make cuts in objectives or limit the way to pursue them. Instead of demonstrating that a hypothesis is always true, one may choose to demonstrate that it is true only under certain conditions, for which convincing tests could be carried out. For example, an effort estimation method could be demonstrably more accurate only for a certain class of systems, such as web-based systems. Thus, the fact that the method has not been tested with other types of systems, such as basic software, embedded systems or electronic games, is not a flaw of the work, but a limitation.

Limitations are, therefore, aspects of the work of which the author is aware and recognizes the importance, but is unable to address in the time available. But this normally only refers to scope, not to incomplete methodological procedures. For example, a limitation saying that the hypothesis was not tested due to lack of time would not be acceptable.

It is important, in research papers, that known limitations are clearly identified by the author from the beginning. This will prevent the author from getting lost in digressions or in the search for aspects that go beyond the initial objectives. This also prevents the reader from creating overly broad expectations about the work, which will later be frustrated.

Again, it is expected that a good interaction with the advisor will help the student to place the necessary limitations on his objectives, so that the work can be successfully completed in the available time.

6.7 Discussion

According to what was seen in this chapter, the research work should be framed in a theme that, as an area of knowledge, should be the researcher's domain. Within the theme, the researcher must establish one or more objectives to be pursued. These objectives must have at least one working hypothesis, which must have a good justification for having been chosen. The methodological procedure will clarify how the hypothesis will be tested by the author of the work, and the limitations will make it clear which aspects will not be addressed.

It is understandable the difficulty of many students who enter, especially in the master's degree, in understanding this structure and carrying out an organized work in this way. Thus, dissertations arise that are often merely a presentation of a system, a proposal tested in only one or two situations, or even dissertations that focus on collecting data and do not adequately elaborate the concepts that the data represent.

This difficulty is especially due to the fact that, perhaps for the first time in his life, the student will be faced with extensive individual work, in which his initiative will be fundamental to success. School work, even in graduation and specialization, is often limited to bibliographic research. The student simply collects material from various sources on an ad hoc basis and organizes this information in a personal way. The structure of scientific research, especially in master's and doctoral programs, goes far beyond bibliographic research, as we have tried to show in this chapter.

Literature review

The literature review for a research work must be very well planned and conducted. One can start the research with a reading of more comprehensive works that give an overview of the whole, and then go deeper into increasingly specific themes.

When a research is carried out in which some Computing technique is applied to some other area of knowledge, it is necessary to review the literature on the technique itself, on the area of application and, above all, on the applications that have already been attempted with this technique or similar techniques in the same or equivalent areas. For example, a student who intends to develop a multi-agent system to assist flight controllers must have a deep understanding of multi-agent systems and the problems that flight controllers face to practice their profession. However, he should not think, as sometimes happens, that this is the first time that someone is going to try to develop a multi-agent system for this type of application. The catapult student mentioned earlier has studied rivers and catapults, but he did not inquire whether anyone had ever tried to cross a river using a catapult. If such research existed and he had access to it, he would have seen that the results were not encouraging and perhaps he would have chosen another research topic before he had devoted most of his master's time to something fruitless.

A monograph on applied research that presents a good bibliographic review of the Computing tool and the application area, but which does not mention any previous attempt to apply this tool in the area suffers from the "forgotten intersection syndrome". A monograph with this problem is possibly reinventing the wheel.

The forgotten intersection syndrome, in general, is justified by students with phrases such as "I haven't found anything similar to what I'm doing". This negative reasoning should be avoided. It must never be said that nothing similar has been found. Something must be presented as a reference. This reference may be more or less similar to the approach used from a relative point of view. But always the most similar approach of all (however less similar it may be) should be sought.

It might be interesting to think like this: "No one has done anything like what I'm doing, but many things have been done by human beings throughout their history. So I could classify things that have already been done in terms of how similar they are to what I'm doing. The things that are closest to my work will be my reference, even if the resemblance is small."

Thus, the empty foundation is avoided, that is, saying that your work is original because no one has ever done anything like it. One should not base an entire research work on denial. You must show what others have done and then show that the work done is different or better than these references.

7.1 Types of Bibliographic Sources

There are several types of bibliographic sources. Each one will have its usefulness in certain moments of the research. Books in general contain more complete, didactic and well-developed information. The purpose of the book is precisely to present a particular area of science in a didactic and well-founded way. Information about future work that leads to research ideas will rarely be found in books.

Some books are specifically dedicated to presenting open problems in certain areas, but most are not. In general, such books are products of scientific events. Most textbooks seek to present only the information that is already consolidated.

Research ideas will be more easily found in articles that are usually published in conferences or journals. Most exact sciences value publication in journals more. The area of Computing, however, has different characteristics in this aspect, since it considers publications in conferences as important, and often even more important, than publications in journals.

This means that, in the area of Computing, good articles can be found both in journals and in conference proceedings. What differences can then be expected? The process of submission and publication in conferences and journals is different. Therefore, different types of articles can be expected in these two vehicles.

Conferences normally have a deadline for paper submission. From a set of submitted and evaluated works, the best ones are sent for publication. In general, some modifications are suggested, but hardly a second round of evaluation is carried out.

In the case of periodicals, there are no deadlines, except in the case of special editions. Articles are submitted, evaluated, and revisions are suggested. Subsequently, the articles are resubmitted, evaluated, and so on. This back-and-forth process can happen multiple times, and it can even take a few years for the article to be published.

The exception is that every rule has an exception, because there are journals that publish articles quickly and events whose demand rate is so high that they will only publish articles of the highest degree of excellence.

The novice researcher in a given area should start the bibliographic review with a more comprehensive literature, which presents him/her with an overview of the area and its research problems under study. The most fundamental concepts can be searched in books, always observing whether it is the most recent edition that is being consulted. One can also examine systematic mappings of the literature, which are publications that aim precisely to present an overview of research in a given area. This type of bibliography presents the researcher with the state of the art of the research area and, possibly, its historical evolution, indicating different developments and the main achievements.

In relation to the other sources, it is possible to differentiate between the classic works and the state of the art. Classic works are those that have been published for a long time and have been cited in many other works. These are works, therefore, with a high impact rate over the years. Whenever the researcher is going to cite some classic concept, he should refer to the most original work. For example, if theory X was formulated by so-and-so in 1975, when a research refers to theory X, it should quote "(So-and-so, 1975)". If Beltrano used this theory in 2017, without producing changes to it, and mentioned it in his work, it would even be possible to quote "(So-and-so, 1975, apud Beltrano, 2017)". But this means that the researcher did not read the 1975 work, but only the secondary reference to it, made in 2017. This should be avoided. If possible, the original work must be sought and studied. If it is not possible, however, to obtain the original work, apud is tolerable, but it should not be used often.

State-of-the-art works are the most recent. These are usually works that still have few citations because they are recent, but they are important because they indicate the most recent achievements in the area and are possibly not yet outdated.

7.2 Critical Reading

Reading scientific works should not be seen only as a learning experience. The researcher must exercise, above all, a critical spirit, to question the validity of the information recorded in the texts that are being read. Passive acceptance of everything that is read does not generate the spirit of searching for new information in the researcher.

For the research topic to become an objective, it is necessary that the reading produces questions. Without questions there are no answers. Many questions that the researcher asks himself while reading a text may not yet have answers and will therefore be excellent candidates for research objectives.

1. Where does the author seem to get his ideas from?
2. What was actually achieved as a result of this work?
3. Could what was done be done differently?
4. If a certain condition were present/absent, would that affect the results?
5. How does this work relate to others in the same area?
6. What would be the next reasonable step to continue this research?
7. Can the results of the work be applied in other areas?
8. What ideas from other areas could be used in this work?

The aforementioned generative questions could also be used to assess the quality of the work being read. In the case of the first question, if it is not possible to find out where the author gets his ideas from, it is likely that this is a weak work, as the ideas must come from bibliographic references or from the observation of phenomena, or else they are hypotheses created by the author, which will be confirmed throughout the work.

In general, authors should not simply write sentences like "Interest in the internet has grown tremendously over the past few years". A statement like this, although at first sight consensual, would need to have a basis. This base can be a reference to another work, which has carried out research on the subject. The basis can also be a statistical survey carried out by the author himself or some company, which demonstrates the validity of the statement. A table or graph with a reliable source would help more than simply stating what was stated in the sentence. Later on, it will also be seen that this specific sentence still has several other problems, such as, for example:

- How is "interest" defined and measured?
- How do you define "to grow a lot"? How is this different from "growing up"?
- What period comprises the "last years"?

Regarding the second generating question, "What was effectively obtained as a result of this work?", if there is no possibility of summarizing the real contribution of the work in a few words, the text is possibly confusing and poorly organized, not making the effective contribution clear. from the article to science.

Regarding the third question, "Could what was done be done in another way?", it leads the reader to ask himself if the approach chosen by the author of the work was correct and adequate. The lack of reliable sampling procedures, for example, can lead the reader to doubt the results. In addition, this question also leads the reader to wonder if other hypotheses could not be studied alternatively in this research.

Regarding the fourth question, "If a certain condition were present/absent, would that affect the results?", it is a great generator of new ideas, since research is often conducted under general conditions of normality. Asking, for example, how the artifact would work under extreme conditions, or in the absence of certain assumed conditions, could lead to interesting questions and, possibly, to research ideas.

Regarding the fifth generating question, "How does this work relate to others in the same area?", it is expected, at first, that the work itself makes this very clear, citing properly and making comparisons with related works. If this is not done, the reader can try to establish relationships between the work read and other works. Often, important aspects about the work (failures) are discovered through these comparisons. Works that only cite related works, but do not make comparisons with what was developed in the work itself, are considered of low quality.

Regarding the sixth triggering question, "What would be a reasonable next step to continue this research?", the answer could be an excellent research objective. Often, research questions are already posed at work by authors in the hope that other groups will continue the research. Just be careful with indications of eminently technical future work, for example, porting the tool to the Web. This is not a research work, it is a technical work.

The seventh question, "Can the results of the work be applied in other areas?", will make the researcher think about special cases of generalization of the work being studied. If it worked for area X, would it also work for area Y? Does an algorithm that compresses text also compress images?

The eighth question, "What ideas from other areas could be used in this work?", brings to the researcher's thinking possible improvements to the work being studied due to related concepts from other research areas, which were possibly not known to the authors of the work. In this way, the successful application of any of these related concepts in the work in question may give rise to an interesting research hypothesis, which, if it has a plausible justification, could be an excellent research objective.

7.3 Research Exposure

In addition to reading, the researcher, in the idea generation phase, must be constantly exposed to a scientific environment. In the case of master's and doctoral students, in the phase of elaborating the research objective, it is essential that they try, at least once a week, to generate a research idea to be discussed with the supervisor.

Regularly, the researcher should read at least the abstracts of articles published in the main journals and events in their area of research. In addition to the abstracts, you should try to read at least one or two articles of greater relevance to the research area.

In addition, whenever possible, the researcher should participate in lectures and seminars in which he can exchange ideas with other researchers, in addition to observing the way of work of other research groups. In the case of master's and doctoral students, this also implies participating, as a listener, in the largest possible number of theses and dissertations defenses, even if they do not refer to their specific area of research. This is important for them to understand how the works are evaluated by the boards.

7.4 Systematic Bibliographic Search

One of the problems that students eventually go through, as already mentioned, is to justify that they did not find anything effectively related to the subject they want to research. Disorganized searches are unlikely to lead to good results or reassure the student when asked: "Hasn't someone already done this?".

One of the best ways to defend yourself against "you didn't look for it right" remarks is to carry out a systematic literature review. The idea is to prepare and document a review protocol so that the process can be repeated independently and produce the same results.

An essential point in a systematic review is the choice of keywords. Very generic choices will produce too many results, making the search difficult. On the other hand, very restrictive terms or the lack of some equivalent terms, such as synonyms, in the search may cause important results not to appear.

Thus, it is expected that the researcher carefully elaborates the list of terms for the search and that, if he is inexperienced, such as a student, request a review by his advisor or someone more experienced, both in the field of work and in carrying out systematic reviews.

That understood, it should also be mentioned that, in relation to the objectives of bibliographic research, one can speak of two types:

- *Systematic review of the literature*(RSL): the objective is to answer very specific research questions about a topic by analyzing the content of a significant number of primary articles (articles that effectively report theoretical or empirical research results). The objective in this case is to reach some conclusion from the study of the content of these articles.

- *Systematic mapping of literature*(MSL): the objective is broader and consists of knowing what research is being done in a given area, without necessarily answering more specific questions. Often, this type of research aims to determine whether any topic is receiving more attention than others, or even if there are gaps in research within a given area.

As can be seen, in the case of RSL, a more restricted set of articles will be sought, and they will be analyzed in depth. In the case of MSL, we usually work with a greater number of articles that are analyzed in a more superficial way.

It is often recommended to do an MSL as a preliminary to an RSL. That is, you will first see an overview of your research area and then choose a focus and answer more closed research questions in this topic.

Systematic review does not eliminate this risk, but it is believed that it can greatly reduce it. Furthermore, the fact that it can be objectively evaluated and even repeated allows one to say how well it was done. A researcher might, for example, look at the search string used and come to the conclusion that it left out some relevant terms, and thus propose a new run of the review. In the case of the ad hoc review, it is much more difficult to know if any work was left out, because there is no parameter to carry out this verification.

7.4.1 Risks

Despite the obvious advantages of the systematic review over the ad hoc review, it also has its risks. The first and possibly the most obvious one is related to the search string. A very generic string will return a very large number of studies, making their examination difficult due to their volume. Thus, in such a situation, there is a risk of abandoning the research due to the impossibility of completing it in a reasonable time. On the other hand, the solution to this risk is to add more terms that make the search more restrictive, that is, terms that are combined with the others by "and" ("and"), which will reduce the amount of results and possibly focus on more relevant articles.

It should be mentioned that usually the terms of a search must be informed in English since most of the relevant research papers are published in this language. Eventually, terms in other languages may be sought, especially when comparing results from works published in different languages. An example of this case can be found in the review by Ramos et al. (2015), which compares the reality of computer education in Brazil in relation to the rest of the world.

But another risk is failing to mention keyword synonyms that might be important in the search string. For example, if you are systematically mapping agile models, a first search string could be "agile AND model", indicating that you want jobs in which the words "agile" and "model" appear simultaneously. However, some works may speak of "agile method" and thus not satisfy the search string. In this case, the solution is to reformulate the search string to "agile AND (model OR method)". As the precedence of AND is higher than that of OR, it will be necessary to use parentheses in the string (provided that the search engine allows it).

Another risk is more related to the content of the works themselves, and that is the case of bias. Thus, it can be dangerous to take data that are the result of publications and combine them to obtain a larger base. It is said of a situation where a researcher "proved" the existence of the paranormal by taking data from several published studies, which alone were not statistically relevant. But when all these data were combined, a large enough body of evidence was produced to statistically prove the phenomenon. The problem in this case is bias, as the researcher did not carry out the research independently, but used data from publications. Now, one can imagine that many researchers have produced these primary researches and that some of them have had promising results and others have not. The problem is that only research with promising results were published; those that did not show this type of result were simply abandoned. Thus, using only published data as a basis for statistical analysis produces a possibly wrong result, as it is biased.

A major risk to systematic search is leaving out important work because of an extremely restrictive search string. One way to mitigate this risk is to list those jobs that are already known to be relevant and verify that all of them are returned at least once during searches. If one or more of these jobs was not returned, it should be checked because the search string left it out and it should be reformulated.

7.4.2 Resources

The first step in carrying out a systematic review is its planning, which must be rigorous and well documented.

First of all, you should check that a systematic review or even a systematic mapping of the topic you are going to address has not already been carried out. Believe me, many studies of this type are done and published around the world. So start by looking for the secondary research available in your area of interest. You may not even need to do the systematic review if you find one already done that answers your questions. Some areas, especially those linked to health sciences, even provide portals1 in which terms used in systematic reviews can be consulted and even reserved. In other words, a researcher can go to one of these portals and tell them that in the coming months they will carry out a systematic review with the terms X, Y and Z. Thus, other researchers avoid carrying out reviews with the same terms over a period of time (usually six months) and wait, if necessary, for the results of the review that is already in progress. This avoids unnecessary repeated work.

Well, once you've determined that in fact there is no published work that meets your information needs, you must decide whether to do a mapping or a review. Opt for mapping if the objective is to know a research topic in its extension; It might be a good option to start with. Do a review, however, if you already have an idea of the scope of the studies and want to collect information on primary studies to answer a specific research question about this content.

Table 7.1 Some of the main sources of publications in Computing

In general, it is not recommended to use Google as a search engine for systematic research because, as its search engine adapts to user preferences, it will not provide the same results for different users or even for the same user at different times. . This makes it impossible to repeat the research and, therefore, its verifiability. However, Google is an excellent tool for locating articles that may not be available for free in the databases. Often these articles can be obtained from the author's personal page or can be requested from him.

They also seek to act as relationship platforms in which researchers can share their publications publicly or privately.

7.4.3 Protocol

The review protocol is a formal document that clearly and objectively sets out the entire review process that will be carried out. It must be written and, preferably, even published (there are specialized websites for this). The existence of a formal written document helps to prevent researchers carrying out the review from deviating from the previously defined path.

It can be argued, however, that over the course of the review it is possible that legitimate changes will be felt to be necessary. To mitigate this issue, it is recommended that reviewers conduct a pilot review, before actually starting work. The pilot review could be, for example, a systematic mapping, or even a complete review, but with reduced scope; for example, considering only articles from a more restricted period, such as a single year. That way, with fewer articles to review, researchers can get an idea of how the full review will take place, and doubts and inconsistencies can be addressed before starting the actual work.

According to Kitchenham and Charters (2007), the review protocol document must contain at least the following elements:

- *Background*. The reason and motivation for carrying out the review.
- The research questions to be answered. Details on the research questions are presented in Chapter 8.
- The search strategy. This topic should contain the search string (keywords) and the data sources, between search engines and specific libraries.

- Criteria for inclusion and exclusion of works. It is recommended that these criteria be tested in the pilot evaluation, if any, so that their interpretation is as homogeneous as possible among researchers.
- The study selection procedures. Indicate how many evaluators will do the work, whether they will address different sources or whether they will replicate the work. Usually, it is recommended that researchers make a division of search sources, so that they do not evaluate the same articles, but that some articles in common are evaluated by more than one evaluator to verify that the inclusion and exclusion criteria are applied in a different way. homogeneous form.
- *Quality assessment procedures and checklists.* Reviewers must develop and record procedures and checklists to assess the quality of the articles studied.
- *Data extraction strategy.* It should be defined how information will be extracted from the articles to answer the research questions. This can include questionnaires, tables and checklists.
- *Summary of extracted data.* It should be informed how the extracted data will be synthesized and presented and whether any meta-analysis will be performed.
- *dissemination strategy.* Indicates how the findings will be disseminated or published.
- Schedule of work.

When the review protocol is designed by researchers with little experience, such as students, for example, it is highly recommended that it be reviewed by a more experienced researcher, such as the supervisor or a senior researcher with in-depth knowledge of the research area.

Inclusion/exclusion criteria such as "only the first 50 articles returned by the search will be analyzed" should be avoided. In this case, for example, if the search returned 1500 articles, and the researcher will only read the first 50, what happens with the other 1450? It is likely that a lot of relevant stuff was left out and possibly a lot of irrelevant stuff appears in the set of the first 50 articles. Ideally, in a case like this, the search string should be refined, with the addition of new "AND", so that it returns a more restricted set of articles that can be effectively analyzed by the researcher.

7.4.4 Execution

Once the protocol has been established, reviewed and agreed among the researchers, the review process can begin. First, the bibliographic sources provided for in the protocol are accessed and the established string is applied to the search engine. At this point, it is necessary to verify that all engines effectively accept operators with AND and OR, whether or not the engines automatically do the search using the plural of words, which in some cases can be important to return all the actually relevant studies, and whether or not they are case sensitive searches or accented words. Fortunately, since most searches turn out to be in English, accentuation isn't usually an issue.

The returned studies are then counted. At this point, the number of studies is no longer expected to be exaggerated, as the search string will have already been tested in the pilot review and refined. However, if this occurs, it will be a case of rethinking the search string to make it more restrictive.

Exclusion criteria that are pretty much standard in most surveys are:

- *duplicate studies.* Different search engines may return the same article from the same vehicle.
- *Older versions of a study.* It may happen that studies are updated after a few years, or even an extended version of an article published at a conference is published in a journal. In these cases, the most recent version of the article is always chosen, eliminating the oldest one.

Then, with a reasonable number of articles selected and duplications eliminated, the researchers should seek to obtain the full texts. Unfortunately, databases do not always make them available for free. If this is not the case, it should be checked whether it is possible to acquire the articles (costs are usually high), or to obtain them for free from a Google search or with the author or from platforms such as Research Gate.

Once obtained, the articles must be read and the quality assessment and data extraction must be performed as specified in the review protocol.

7.4.5 Quality Assessment of Studies

Kitchenham and Charters (2007) present an interesting list of questions to assess the quality of studies, especially applicable if they are of a qualitative type, which corresponds to a large amount of work in computing. Some of them are summarized below:

- Are the findings believable?
- If yes, are they relevant?
- How was knowledge extended from the research?
- How well does the assessment validate the initial objectives?
- How well is the scope for generalizing the results explained?

- How well was the composition and coverage of an eventual sample described?
- How well was the data collection done?
- How clear are the links between data, interpretation and conclusions?

The main reason for evaluating the quality of primary studies is to establish a cut-off point to remove studies whose quality is considered insufficient from the research. But it can also be used to see if studies with different levels of quality point to different results.

- Was the data analysis appropriate?
- Was a sensitivity analysis performed?
- Was the sample size adequate?
- Was the selection of the elements to be studied made randomly or for convenience?
- Were the results confirmed by appropriate statistical techniques, such as hypothesis testing?

The set of quality assessment questions can be reused between different systematic reviews. In this case, it is considered a document in its own right and called a "quality instrument". This helps to capitalize on experiences and evolve the quality of systematic reviews carried out in the future.

Finally, an important tool for evaluating the results of review data extraction (not the quality of primary studies) is sensitivity analysis. This technique is applied by subdividing the set of primary studies into subsets, based on some criterion such as, for example, the quality of the studies, type of publication vehicle, type of research method used, etc. It must be verified that the extraction of data from these subsets presents the same results that it presented for the complete set. If they present this property, then it can be concluded that the results are robust, that is, they do not vary from subset to subset. Otherwise, there may be some aspect of the research that has not been correctly identified.

Research Questions

We reserve this chapter to delve into a subject that is fundamental in any scientific research work: the choice of research questions.

Often, students start work with a vague research idea. As long as this idea is not objectively formulated, it is unlikely that much progress will be made in answering any question. This is what happens, for example, when the student focuses only on the product of the work, that is, on the system, algorithm, process, mechanism, but this product is not accompanied by science, that is, an advance in human knowledge.

In the same way as in Easterbrook et al. (2008), possibilities of research questions will be presented based on examples and a classification that Easterbrook et al. adapted from Meltzoff (1998).

Imagine a master's student who is starting his research. He's no catapult fanatic, but he still doesn't have a very precise idea of what he's going to do. He notes that the company where he works has recently started to organize work in self-managed agile teams. There is a feeling that, despite some complications, the work has flowed better. So he would like to do research to prove that self-managed teams are a better option than teams led by a manager.

This is not yet a research question, because it is very vague. Watch:

- What does "better" mean in this context? How is this measured?
- What are self-managed teams effectively? Are there subtypes to consider?
- Same for teams with a manager. It is known that there are several styles of management, ranging from the dictator manager to the facilitator, passing through the

coordinator. Can these subtypes influence a possible comparison with self-managed teams?

Therefore, the following subsections explore possible better research questions that could be produced from this desire to better understand whether working with self-managed teams is better than the more usual ways with a manager coordinating the team's work.

There is no point in carrying out a systematic review that is perfectly planned and executed, but whose research questions do not add anything relevant to human knowledge. Thus, the choice of research questions is fundamental for the quality of a systematic review.

If the researcher is going to do a systematic mapping, he can work with more generic or more granular questions, such as:

- What are the most used techniques or approaches for this or that process?
- Which properties of a given artifact are most studied?
- What are the types of methodological procedure most used in research in area X.

But note that these are not yet questions that will advance human knowledge. They only indicate how the panorama of a certain area is. As can be seen, the mapping does not necessarily extract data from the object of the primary searches; it works more like a map, so you can get to know a specific area of research better.

The systematic literature review is used to answer much deeper questions about research results. Kitchenham and Charters (2007) propose an adaptation for software engineering of the guidelines of the National Health and Medical Research Council of Australia. They thus suggest research questions of the following types:

- Evaluate the effect of a technology.
- Assess the frequency or reason for a project development factor, such as the adoption of a particular technology, or the frequency or rate of success or failure of projects.
- Identify cost and risk factors associated with a technology.
- Identify the impact of technology on reliability and cost models.
- Analyze cost/benefit for employing specific development technologies or software applications.

Kitchenham and Charters (2007) go on to state that a key aspect of literature review is asking the right questions. In this sense, the right questions would be those that have some importance and meaning, both for researchers and for workers in the software industry.

Good research questions, if answered, could lead to changes in the way companies and researchers work; for example, demonstrating that one technique or approach is better than another. It is also possible that the survey results will determine that the currently dominant techniques are better, which bolsters confidence in their application.

Furthermore, good research questions, if answered, may show that current beliefs are incorrect or at least incomplete in relation to reality. In this sense, the work of Tolfo and Wazlawick (2008) can be mentioned, which demonstrated that, to assess whether a company has a favorable environment for agile culture (XP, specifically), it is not enough to assess the visible culture, as was believed, but it was also necessary to look at deeper levels of organizational culture.

In this case, it was a hybrid research that initially evaluated the literature that it was believed that the observation of the company's visible culture was enough to determine its suitability for the agile culture. In a second moment, a case study carried out with six companies that apparently had these favorable conditions, but failed to adopt an agile culture, demonstrated that these factors were not enough, and that the participants' deepest convictions (human factors) needed to be addressed. evaluated and not just the technical factors usually observed.

According to Petticrew and Roberts (2005), a research question should be structured based on the following elements:

- *Population*. What are the individuals (people or artifacts) that we want to analyze? For example, experienced or novice programmers, large or small companies, free or proprietary software.
- *Intervention*. The intervention has to do with the tool/technique/approach/etc. that is used and evaluated. For example, automated testing, agile teams, development effort estimation, etc.
- *Comparation*. Comparison is the verification that is done on whether the tool/technique/approach/etc. studied is better than those currently used. In general, the current technique is described as "traditional", but this term is ill-suited. It is suggested, when applicable, to use the term "control". For example, if the work is going to show the advantages of developing software with self-managed teams, then the control will be teams with managers. Avoid comparing the use of a technique with the use of no technique. For example, it makes sense to compare the use of a new analysis tool with market (control) tools. But it makes no sense to compare the work of someone using a new tool with the work of someone using no tool at all. In this case, the control is inadequate, as there are already tools on the market,

- *Results.* They consist of what you want to measure or improve using comparison. For example, the number of bugs reported, code performance efficiency, total cost of software production, average maintenance time to fix defects, etc.
- *Context.* This aspect can define specific groups of interest for the research. For example, certain research is only interested in self-managing teams in small and medium-sized companies. Thus, large companies are left out of this context and are excluded from the research.
- *experiment design.* It may be the case, depending on the type of results you want, to restrict the set of primary works according to the type of research performed. For example, you can eliminate all articles that do not apply statistical tests to assess the reliability of their results. It should be noted, however, that this can often create research bias and therefore should be done very carefully.

One way of elaborating the search string is to take each of the elements listed above and represent it by a list of synonyms linked by "OR". The lists of synonyms for each of the elements would be linked together by "AND".

That said, it can still be reinforced that it is useless to have well-structured and well-defined questions, but whose answer does not produce any practical effect in research or in the application of Computing in society. Bibliographic research is not an end in itself, but a means to reach relevant and interesting conclusions that may be useful to researchers or the industry.

8.2 Exploratory Questions

Easterbrook et al. (2008) indicate that, initially, the researcher will be able to formulate exploratory questions to begin to better understand the universe of his research. Note that these questions can usually be answered through systematic literature searches. Thus, the authors indicate at least three types of exploratory questions, which are summarized in Table 8.1.

Table 8.1 Exploratory questions

Type	Question format	Examples
existential questions	Is there X?	Do self-managed teams exist? At where? Is there any literature on self-managed teams?
Descriptive and classification questions	How is X? What are your properties? How can X be categorized? How can you measure X? What is your purpose? What are its components? How do the components relate to each other? What are the types of X?	What types of self-managed teams are there? What are the conditions for a team to be considered self-managed? How can we measure the productivity of software development teams? Why do companies employ self-managed teams? What are the roles in a self-managed team?
Descriptive-comparative questions	How does X differ from Y?	What differentiates self-managed teams from teams with managers?

8.3 Descriptive Questions

After having understood his research area a little more in depth, the researcher will be able to elaborate questions that aim to verify the frequency or distribution of some phenomenon that he intends to investigate. For example, out of every 100 agile teams, how many are self-managed? Without elaborating this type of question, it will be difficult to state things like "often", "in most cases", etc. These are statements that a researcher can only make if they have been the result of some study, but not based solely on intuition.

The suggestions of types of descriptive questions, still according to Easterbrook et al. (2008), are presented in Table 8.2.

Table 8.2 Descriptive questions

Type	Question format	Examples
Frequency and distribution issues	How often does X occur? What is the average amount of X?	What is the ratio of self-managed teams in the industry to managed teams? Are self-managed teams more common in small or large companies?
Descriptive questions of processes	How does X normally work? What is the process by which X occurs? In what sequence do the events of X occur? What steps does X go through as it evolves? How does X achieve its purpose?	How do self-managed teams work? How does a managed team become self-managed?
relationship issues	How are X and Y related? Do the occurrences of X correlate with those of Y?	Are self-managed teams more productive than managed teams? Is the level of satisfaction of members of self-managed teams higher than that of teams with a manager?

The researcher begins to better understand their research space at this point. Here it can already be seen that more often it will be necessary to carry out experiments, especially in the case of relationship issues. But it will still be possible to discover many answers with bibliographic or documentary reviews.

8.4 Causality Issues

It is not enough, however, to know that two phenomena are related, as this does not necessarily explain cause and effect. For example, it could be observed that self-managed teams are more productive than teams with managers. But from this one cannot conclude that self-management increases productivity. What could be happening is that teams that are highly productive end up choosing to become self-managing and, in this case, it is not the form of organization that increases productivity, but the productivity that leads to a new form of organization.

There are websites that show the most absurd yet true correlations, such as one that shows a high correlation between US investments in science and technology and the number of suicides by hanging. This correlation exists primarily because, over the years, both values have increased as the population and economy have grown. The problem with correlations is that if you look hard enough for something that correlates with a dataset you already have, you'll end up finding it. But that doesn't prove cause-effect.

There are even more absurd cases, such as the research that shows that 99% of people who committed violent crimes had eaten bread up to 24 hours before the crime. The problem here is that, in fact, almost all people eat bread, and the few who commit violent crimes are very likely to have eaten bread in the near past. Again, there is nothing about cause and effect to be found here.

A more controversial situation is related to research that seeks to determine whether violent games incite young people to violence. This concern began when it was discovered that the perpetrators of a school massacre in the USA were playing a famous game in which the objective was to kill any being that came their way. At first, this correlation seemed obvious: violent games provoke violence. But it has not been noted that the number of young people who play violent games is also very large and are not violent in real life. Without wanting to enter into a moral discussion, but remaining exclusively in the sphere of analysis of numbers, research in this line has presented inconclusive or contradictory results.

Causality issues, then, according to Easterbrook et al. (2008) are shown in Table 8.3.

Another example, related to issues of comparative causal interaction, is a study that showed that only experienced programmers do better when they use delegation techniques rather than centralization (the control technique). It was observed that, in the case of novice programmers, the control technique worked better than the delegation technique. Thus, delegation works best with experienced programmers and centralization with novice programmers.

Table 8.3 Causality issues

Type	Question format	Examples
Causality issues	X cause Y? X prevent Y? What causes Y? What are all the factors that cause Y? What effect does X have on Y?	Do highly productive teams tend to become self-managed? What makes a team self-managed? What are the factors that make a team produce better? What effects does management style have on a team's productivity?
Comparative causality issues	X causes more Y than Z? X is it better to prevent Y than Z?	Do self-managed teams handle changes in requirements better than other teams? Do teams that become self-managed improve their productivity? Do teams that become self-managed produce products with fewer bugs?
Comparative causal interaction issues	X or does Z cause more Y under some circumstances but not under others?	Do self-managed teams handle changes in requirements better than other teams only when they are made up of experienced people, but not otherwise?

It is common in Computing, and especially in software engineering, to ask questions about how to achieve a certain objective. While most of the questions in the previous sections are concerned with just observing how things are, the design questions seek to answer how things could be.

Thus, Table 8.4 presents a summary of questions of this type.

Design questions, however, do not dispense with questions about knowledge, correlations, etc. identified before. In order to give a consistent answer to design questions, it is usually necessary to have a good knowledge of the area and the existing techniques. Therefore, the research starts with exploratory questions, then goes through the explanations of the current situation to finally arrive at questions about how the situation could or should be.

Table 8.4 Design Questions

Type	Question format	Examples
design issues	What is an effective way to get X? What strategies help get X?	What is the most effective way to deploy self-managed teams? What factors influence the success or failure of self-managed teams?

Critical Analysis of Research Proposals

Between 2001 and 2008, in the research methodology discipline of the Graduate Program in Computer Science at the Federal University of Santa Catarina (UFSC), dozens of incoming students were invited to present a seminar with a research proposal. The presentations were used to help the students to perceive problems in their proposals and to improve them. In this chapter we will analyze some texts contained in these proposals before their improvement, that is, the texts presented are material not reviewed by the students. Thus, it was considered appropriate not to mention the name of the authors of this material, with the text that was produced by the students being placed with indentation, followed by the comments.

9.1 Analysis of Contextualization and Research Problem Placement

In this section texts referring to the contextualization of the problem are analyzed. The evaluation verifies that the problem is, in fact, a research problem and that it is very clear. The results are presented below.

One of the great difficulties that the academic encounters when entering a university is to face the discipline of Research Methodology. It does not know ABNT and its norms, as well as the proposals for formatting and structuring a research report. To alleviate the problem, we intend to develop a multimedia system, using techniques related to the development of systems of this type, such as software ergonomics, a support method to improve user-machine interaction and the distribution of resources in the system.

Even supposing that this is a real problem, it would still be possible to ask why the student considers that a multimedia system will be a solution. Are there no other possibilities? Here it seems that the tool has already been chosen without analyzing the problem itself in detail. Also, weren't there already multimedia tools for this purpose? At this point, at least a systematic mapping of the literature would be in order to verify if the problem exists and which solutions have already been proposed.

It should be considered, in cases like this, that the observation of the problem may be located, as in the case of the student who observed that the river that crossed the city where he lived could not be crossed. The problem referred to may then be a consequence of the teaching techniques of a particular teacher that the student has observed, and not be a generalized problem that affects all educational institutions.

In the Information Technology Department at [...] there is no specific method for managing outsourced software development projects. Outsourced software development projects have been delivered late and with requirements not being fully met.

The problem concerns a specific company. If that company doesn't use a method to manage projects, then a more obvious solution is to implement some existing method that has already been tested, that is, it is technical work, not scientific.

This problem, in the way it is presented, does not justify a research proposal, as, for example, in this case, in which the development of a method for managing outsourced workers would be proposed. It remains to indicate why the existing methods would not do the job.

The system [...] is made up of 14 higher education [...] institutions. There has been no increase in the number of these institutions, but the institutions are expanding. The number of students enrolled has been increasing year by year. The information will be taken from the socioeconomic questionnaire and from the academic secretariat, which form a large database, enabling the use of data mining in this database.

There is an opportunity here, not a problem. The opportunity is the existence of data in abundance, so it is proposed to do data mining on this data. It remains to inform what is intended to discover when analyzing the data or, at least, what clue is being followed. As the Laughing Cat said to Alice, "For those who don't know where they're going, any road will do."

*octrees*are used for spatial representation of scenarios and objects. They are used because they allow the quick determination of non-visible parts. They need infinite precision to represent curves (distort reality).

Here we have a good example of contextualization. The message is quick, but it poses a problem clearly. Even if the reader does not know what octrees are, the author informs that they are used for spatial representation of scenarios and objects. In addition, the author informs that they suffer from a serious problem: they need infinite precision, which does not exist in computing. Thus, research possibilities related to this problem can be explored. However, the research questions still need to be formulated.

Distributed services have been used to achieve transparency, performance and reliability in systems. Among the problems encountered is the difficulty in obtaining high reliability with minimal loss of performance.

Here the student presents a clear cost-benefit relationship: it is difficult to improve reliability without losing performance. The initial statement, however, is somewhat generic and could be more detailed.

Application of case-based reasoning (RBC) in weather forecasting. Use of past cases (time) in the search for a possible solution (forecast).

No problem was identified here. Weather forecast is just the theme. Apparently, the student has already chosen the tool (RBC) and now wants to see how it works. But it did not specify the problem or justify the choice of tool.

An electrical system is composed of several components that need to be shut down for maintenance during a certain period: generators, transmission line, etc. The functioning of the electrical system can be represented by equations that represent the physical limitations of the components. The problem is to apply maximizing the maximum load served in various scenarios. The system must consider the stochastic model related to the reservoirs.

It seems that the student confuses the problem with the objective. Maximizing the load served seems to be the desired goal, but what is the real problem? Are there no mathematical methods or systems for doing this maximization? If so, what limitations do they suffer from? These limitations, which possibly exist, would be the real research problem.

Computational reflection is a widely recognized mechanism for adapting and reconfiguring software at runtime.

Notice how the adverb "widely" can be dispensed with from the sentence without impairing the sense of it. Otherwise, this is merely information, not a problem.

3-D reconstruction is critical in many application domains and is researched today for accuracy (accuracy), precision (completeness and level of detail) and performance (speed), where the problem is to find the 3-D geometry corresponding to parts of the observed scene or the whole of it. In the current state of development of the area, there is no general theory that unifies the problem. Therefore, studies are carried out in specific contexts and applying restrictions. Thus, there are approaches that use multiple views of the scene, some prior knowledge of the object, indexing by image aspects, etc. The union and improvement of some of these approaches is a promising field of research.

Contextualization limits the problem well. The statement that there is no general theory of the area must be justified by a bibliography that makes this statement or by a study by the author himself in which, from a systematic mapping of the literature, he arrives at the conclusion that such a theory is effectively non-existent. . The student clearly indicates a field of research, but not necessarily yet a research problem. As the area is characterized by several approaches that complement each other, it is possible to try to make junctions and improvements between the different theories. It would be necessary, possibly, to define what would be the gains of these approaches. Efficiency? Efficiency? Or just a better knowledge area organization? GIS (Geographical Information System). The integration of geographic and alphanumeric data is still a major challenge. The manipulated data is commonly part of a larger system. Interoperability is critical.

The text was originally structured in topics. Here it is possible to clearly perceive a problem: interoperability between textual database systems and geographic data systems. It remains to characterize this as a research problem and not as a technical problem. As it stands, it seems to be just a technical challenge to solve this case. Most MSEs do not have a defined process. Limitations of human and financial resources for the adoption of dense processes or consulting services. Agile processes promise simplicity and performance for small teams, but empirical evidence of applications in MSEs is scarce. Agile processes do not clearly show all the cycles of their process.

The first statement about micro and small enterprises (MSEs) would need a bibliographic or empirical foundation. The statement about the scarcity of empirical evidence of applications of agile processes in MSEs does not necessarily imply a research problem. It would also be necessary to identify some special characteristic of these MSEs that would make them different from other companies in relation to the adoption of agile methods.

XML has been widely used in electronic data interchange (EDI), which has increased interest in handling persistent XML data. Researches developed in native XML DBs have sought to reach the "state of the art" in the management of semi-structured data.

The alleged increase in interest in an area (which would need to be justified by recent bibliographic evidence) does not imply the existence of a research problem, but only a research topic.

One of the biggest problems in distributing videos to mobile devices is their low availability. Using a shorter time to transfer videos, there is better use of the connection bandwidth and savings in battery consumption, which have limited capacity. Grid is a secure version of Web Services for sharing data and resources (Foster, 2001). Entities like OGSI and WSRF define specifications for toolkits where we have user control, security and open interface to ensure compatibility. In this way, we can propose a mesh of video servers in which a client application can copy video fragments from different points, providing high availability of resources and reducing the overhead existing in a centralized system.

Some heterogeneous XML data source integration processes define a single conceptual schema (global schema) representative of the schema of all these sources. Through this global schema, it is possible to perform queries transparently, since it abstracts the complexities inherent to data sources, such as structural and semantic differences. Works like [...] deal with this problem.

Although the text mentions it, it does not present a problem, but a solution. The referenced text apparently presents solutions for the combination of heterogeneous XML bases. So, it remains for the author of the research proposal to identify a problem, possibly in the referenced work, that deserves attention to be solved. By simply reading the previous text, it is not possible to know which problem will be solved in the monograph.

In supermarkets, for example, there is a need to predict the amount of products that will be sold in a range of time, in order to optimize the quantity purchased, reducing costs and logistical needs. Therefore, time series forecasting was studied, which has statistical models that have been used in the market. These, however, sometimes do not perfectly contemplate the objectives, sometimes they require many resources to do so, therefore, there is a need to find a model that more appropriately meets this case. Some studies in neural networks suggest that there is a possibility that this model will be found in this field of research.

The text poses a real problem, mentions that existing solutions have limitations and proposes to research a way to overcome them using a tool that, according to the author, the literature presents as a trend. However, if neural networks have already been used for this purpose, it will be necessary to compare the results of existing models with the model defined by the author.

Web Services have been widely used in order to provide interoperability between applications. Some applications need the services accessed to be highly available, that is, active and in operation for as long as possible.

This is a description of a need. In order for it to become a research problem, it is necessary to indicate how this need has been met and what are the limitations of current techniques.

There is an increasing number of machines connected to the internet. Increasingly capable machines. Studies have shown that 93% of computer processing capacity remains idle. This capability can be used to process projects that require high computational performance at a low operating cost. The environment [...] is an alternative for this.

Here, the information presented, idle machines on the internet, is quantified and based on a bibliographic study (although it is not explicitly cited). However, this text does not present a research problem, but an opportunity. Idle machines are an opportunity to take advantage of their processing potential, but it remains to be established what new knowledge one seeks to generate at work.

Jurisprudence (Latin: juris prudentia) is a legal term with several meanings. The most common refers to the application of legal case studies in judicial decision-making. Thus, "jurisprudence" can refer to "law based on cases" or the legal decisions that have developed and that accompany statutes in the application of laws in factual situations. Much of the legal knowledge is formatted in documents that contain decisions rendered in sentences or judgments. The research aims to contribute to define a model of research architecture in documents with semantic meaning incorporated, creating a connection between the legal technical language and its representation, using ontologies suitable for its processing in tools that help in the refinement of knowledge.

This contextualization presents a well-defined theme, but fails to characterize the research problem. The proposal is to define a research architecture model, but it does not establish what are the problems with any existing research architectures. Even the mention of a direct application in the legal field does not allow concluding that this work is unprecedented, as this type of application possibly already existed at the time of elaboration of this proposal. A systematic mapping of the literature will be important here. Even if it did not exist, it should be made clear what makes this domain different from others and why other systems prior to the one that will be proposed would not work.

The exploration of oil wells involves a very high degree of uncertainty, and this uncertainty generates high risks in terms of costs. In order to carry out this risk analysis, the simulation technique has been used, requiring knowledge of the distributions of the time values of the operations. For the discovery of these distributions, there are several methods that evaluate adherence to some probability model. But for that, it is necessary that there is a historical series of times of similar operations. When there is no such history, how to discover probability models?

Here, contextualization presents a real problem: to carry out a simulation, it is necessary to have a historical series. The problem is raised of how to do this simulation when a series is not available, which in fact can happen. It remains now to formulate a good hypothesis.

9.2 General Purpose Analysis

This section seeks to assess whether a general objective is well written, whether it is a research objective and whether it is clear that it can be verified at the end of the work. Special attention is given to the verb that presents the objective. It is also analyzed whether the objective presented clearly defines a scientific research or a technological objective, such as, for example, the implementation of a system. The results are presented below.

Develop a hypermedia system observing ergonomic criteria and design principles to support the teaching of scientific methodology.

Achieve reliability through replication with five servers, achieving a maximum loss of 20% of performance compared to a system without replication.

The objective is clear: "to obtain reliability". It remains to be specified, however, how reliability is measured so that it can be concluded at the end of the work if it was obtained. The proposed comparison with a system without replication would imply that the technique in question has not yet been explored in other works.

The general objective of this work is to develop, implement and evaluate the impact of an approach for the management of outsourced software development projects in an electricity transmission company.

The first two verbs, "develop" and "implant", are technical rather than research objectives. The third verb, "evaluate", points to a research objective, but "impact" is too subjective to be evaluated. There should be better specification of what you want to find out, otherwise you may be looking for nothing.

Study AI techniques, more specifically RBC. Demonstrate the efficiency of using RBC in weather forecasting. Development of a prototype for demonstration of results.

The first sentence cannot be a search objective. At least, not from scientific research. The student will study AI techniques, but he does this to supply knowledge that he does not yet have. This knowledge is, however, already in the public domain. Therefore, this study does not produce new knowledge and cannot be presented as a research objective.

The second sentence is already better. Something will be demonstrated. However, it is not very clear where this objective is intended to go. How to measure efficiency? Will it be compared with some other technique?

The development of the prototype, presented in the third sentence, is a step of the work, and the prototype can be an interesting by-product, but it does not seem to be a real research objective.

The objective is to develop a method of refinement of the 3-D reconstruction, through an adaptive memory of the already reconstructed objects, so that new analyzed objects are stored and those already known are refined. Thus, (hypothesis) there may be greater completeness and increased accuracy of the reconstruction, given the cumulative nature of the process. It is a memory with an implicit geometric representation, through indexing/mapping of objects from aspects of the image, such as contours, etc.

Developing a method can be a good research objective, although sometimes students confuse method, process, procedure, mechanism, architecture, system, etc. In this case, in fact, it is a method involving computer graphics techniques. There is a clear hypothesis, which consists of a technique to be used: adaptive memory. There is a clear objective associated with this hypothesis, which is to obtain greater completeness and accuracy in the 3-D reconstruction. For the objective to be complete, it would only be necessary to indicate how much the current methods are able to obtain in terms of accuracy and completeness, so that it can be known, at the end of the project, if the attempted technique improved these values.

Identify the most relevant aspects that influence the performance of reflective systems.

"Identifying" something can be a research objective as long as it is clear what you are trying to identify. This text, in question, could be improved, as it has several words with subjective connotations. For example, how do you judge that one aspect is more relevant than another? What does it mean to influence performance? Is the presence of a virus on the computer, for example, an aspect that should be considered? It can affect the performance of a reflective system, as well as other systems. In this way, the number of aspects can be arbitrarily large. In addition, just identifying something may be insufficient to have a concrete and useful result. The objective could be complemented with the proposition of some technique to overcome the identified problems, moving from the purely descriptive scope to the design scope.

Classify students on their academic performance. Classify students according to their financial need. To compare the school performance of graduates [sic] by SAEM and vestibular. Predict the academic performance of students at the university. Predict cases of change of institution. Assist in decision making.

The first three sentences are well connected and point to a clear research objective. However, this objective does not seem to be a Computer Science objective. Possibly, the student intended to use computerized systems to make the comparison, but this is not enough. There must be a production of useful knowledge for the area of Computing. Otherwise, the master's can and should be attempted in another area. The fourth and fifth sentences do not seem to easily follow the first three. It is not clear how, from the performance of students and their financial situation, it will be possible to predict their school performance and what would happen if they changed institutions. The last sentence is more of an expected result than a monograph objective. If the objective stated in the first three sentences was achieved,

Develop an algorithm based on the relaxation of Lagrangian variables to determine the optimal scale of maintenance of an electrical system.

An algorithm based on relaxation of Lagrangian variables seems to be a good solution to optimize something, for example, the maintenance of an electrical system. But why not other techniques? Are there any techniques currently being used? What results does it produce? How much do you want to improve and to what extent? Note that the student's real objective is to obtain an optimal scale of maintenance in an electrical system; developing an algorithm is a means to achieve this goal.

Generate surface approximation on external octree nodes.

This is a succinct objective. Perhaps that is why it is difficult to determine whether it is suitable as a research objective. At first, generating a surface approximation does not bring new knowledge to the fore. It is an activity, not a research objective. It could be rewritten perhaps as "demonstrating that it is possible to generate surface approximation...". This is if until the moment of the research it had never been done. Otherwise, the wheel could be reinvented.

Develop a hospital management system that, based on workflow technology, allows the modeling and execution of medical processes, interacting with data servers in the standard [...].

Developing a system, however good it may be, will never be a research objective. The system can be used to demonstrate something, but the system itself is a technical objective.

Offer a solution for planning navigation routes for a semi-known environment. Apply this solution to a neurosurgical planning system. Demonstrate that this solution is correct by comparing it with other methods currently used (manual!).

"Offer solution" is fine as an expected result, but there are many ways to do this. You can buy a system, you can implement an algorithm, you can even create a whole new theory and practice in this area, with a view to providing a solution.

So this would have to be better defined. The application of this solution in a certain area can be interesting, especially if the current methods used are manual. There must be a bibliographic reference or the presentation of research that demonstrates that the current technique is in fact inadequate. A quick observation at the local hospital would not be sufficient justification.

Propose a model for identifying characteristics for a stratified sampling plan.

"To propose" is a verb that is used in many monographs as an objective, but it is a dangerous verb if it is not accompanied by a relevant direct object. In the previous case, what is being proposed is a model for identifying characteristics. Okay, the model can be proposed. But it is necessary to clearly indicate what happens with other models that possibly must exist. If they don't exist, you should evaluate why they don't exist and reference the models most similar to what you intend to propose.

In short, one cannot arrive and simply propose something. A good justification for such a proposal must be presented.

Port the system to the UC Berkeley WSN architecture.

Unless the process of "porting" presents challenges that imply the construction of new knowledge in computing, the work, as proposed, is just a technical objective that could be performed by a professional in the area, without him being, at the end of it, , awarded the title of Master.

The objective of this work is to present a systematic mechanism that, through contracts defined in OCL notation, generates collaboration diagrams, applying design patterns.

It would be necessary to know the area well to know that the proposed mechanism does not exist; therefore, the student should have said this clearly in the context. Furthermore, the contextualization would have to demonstrate that there is some advantage in creating collaboration diagrams from OCL contracts. This done, the objective can be accepted as a research objective.

9.3 Analysis of Specific Objectives

Specific objectives should reflect by-products or a breakdown of the main objective. In principle, steps that are merely intermediate to reach the general objective should not be mentioned as a specific objective. Several other precautions must also be taken, according to the comments in the following examples.

1. Use software ergonomics criteria.
2. Apply design principles in the development of multimedia systems.
3. Develop a user-friendly interface in a multimedia system, that is, easy to use, apply and communicate.
4. Adapt the system to a support method for authoring systems.

Every objective must have a verb, but it must indicate the production of some new knowledge. This goes for specific goals as well. Objective 1 is presented with the verb "utilizar", which does not lend itself well to a research objective, because the fact that the author is using something does not mean that he is producing some kind of new knowledge. This goes for objective 2. Objective 3 really implies something being done, possibly something new. However, you may need to measure what it means to be user-friendly and easy to use. Some criteria for measuring these characteristics should be mentioned. Objective 4 does not seem to be research, but technological: there is a system that will be adapted.

1. Techniques to identify patterns in characteristic.
2. Clustering techniques.
3. Categorization of continuous variables.
4. Discretization.

For these items to correspond to specific objectives there should initially be a verb in each item. As they are, it is not possible to conclude that they would be achievable.

1. Develop data replication method between servers.
2. Show limitations of existing methods for replicating load-balanced servers.

1. Analyze outsourced software project management methods.
2. Develop a customized method to manage the cost, schedule, quality and risk aspects of projects.
3. Adapt or develop a software tool (if no suitable one exists) to support the application of the method.
4. Deploy the method.
5. Collect and analyze empirical data, resulting from the application of the method in projects.
6. Propose improvements in the developed method.

Here the confusion that is often established between specific objectives, methodological procedure and schedule of activities clearly appears. Specific objectives should be measurable end results, usually a breakdown or by-product of the overall objective. But the student practically presents a sequence of steps that lead to the general objective. It is not a methodological procedure, as it would need to be complemented with other information, but what was presented is a list of activities on which the work schedule would possibly be built. One can even speak of intermediate objectives of each stage of the research process, but several of them are not research objectives, but technical activities.

1. Implement system boot and hardware abstractions for [...] on [...].
2. Define, implement, test and evaluate a family of communication protocols from [...].

3. Define, implement, test and evaluate an energy resource control system for [...].
4. Define and implement applications that allow the evaluation of implemented systems.

Here, the division of the problem into sub-problems is even adequate, but the activities of defining, implementing and testing are not research objectives, but technical objectives.

1. Minimization of the object occlusion problem.
2. Reduction of reconstruction time, given the option to obtain the shape of the object by classifying 2-D aspects, if it is already known.

Here are two valid specific goals. Only that, in the case of the first, a metric would be needed to measure the problem of occlusion of objects so that one can know if it has been minimized.

1.
2. Determine inflection points in octrees.
3. Generate bitmaps from octree nodes.
4. Determine normal vectors in octree nodes for lighting.

The first objective differs from the others because it does not have an associated verb. The others seem more like activities to be carried out in pursuit of the general objective, but they would not be specific objectives, just steps.

9.4 Analysis of Justification of the Hypothesis

The justification of a research paper has at least two parts:

- *Justification of the problem*. It indicates why this research is worth doing and what can be improved or discovered if the research is done.

- *Justification of the hypothesis.* Indicates evidence that the working hypothesis is promising.

Thus, the student who presents a research proposal must refer to these two aspects, that is, he must justify the importance of the research problem and, also, the choice of the working hypothesis. Usually, the importance of the research problem will have already been addressed in the context of the problem. Next, some justifications produced in monograph proposals are analyzed, with the idea that they would be hypotheses justifications.

The efficiency of a stratified sampling plan depends on the empirical knowledge and experience of the researcher. The proposed method will assist in the development of the sampling plan, identifying strata that will provide greater precision.

Here the student presents an expected advantage for the proposed method, but does not justify the research hypothesis in the sense that would be expected. He should make it clear, from the identification of the problem, which were the tried solutions tested, where they failed and, finally, in the justification, explain why he believes that the approach he proposes can be successful. Current replication methods generate a lot of network traffic and reduce parallelism between them. If there is no need for parallelism, replication can be done much faster and with less load on the network.

It is a good justification as it presents a limitation related to existing methods and justifies, based on that, a potential solution, explaining why it would be suitable.

Currently, there is no method for monitoring outsourced software development projects adapted to the reality of public companies. With the adoption of a method that allows the management of outsourced software development projects, it will be possible to better control the progress of projects, allowing the verification of deviations and decision-making to correct them in a timely manner.

Lack of software that allows specialists to model the hospital process based on their experience and that is capable of executing and managing the modeled process, including controlling the allocation of resources. Lack of standardization in medical data, making diagnoses difficult and compromising or making statistical calculations impossible.

Here again the student tries to justify his work by the absence of certain things. Software is lacking in several areas, but the construction of software does not always imply a research activity. This goes for patterns.

9.5 Analysis of Methodological Procedure

Below, some proposed methodological procedures are analyzed, as presented. All analyzes are based on extremely summarized versions of the proposals, that is, enough to fill a transparency sheet. So all of them need more detail when they are transformed into the text of the research proposal or the final work. Thus, the analysis will consider issues related to the methodological procedure at its most abstract level.

Initially, it is considered recommended that the methodological procedure is only defined when the research objective is already known. He must then show how the proponent is going to do so that his working hypothesis is tested and that, in the end, it can be concluded whether or not it is true.

1. Bibliographic survey on the topics covered in this work, such as: ergonomic criteria, interactivity, authorship support method and others.
2. Research on the support method to be used.
3. Definition of audiovisual resources to be used in the work.
4. System modeling according to the chosen authorship support method.
5. Development of the multimedia tool.
6. System tests.

The method starts with the bibliographic survey (steps 1 and 2), but does not establish whether it will be a review or a mapping, nor what research questions are being sought. Steps 3 and 4 are linked to what the student will discover in the literature review and, therefore, cannot be more specific. Steps 5 and 6 are so generic that they would serve a very wide range of monograph proposals. The question is how the research hypothesis will be tested. This method does not make it clear.

1.
2. Adding knowledge to the engine.
3. Experiments + bibliographic research = monograph.

Here the student seems to propose a style of project in which he will evaluate a certain hypothesis, the use of knowledge or design patterns, against the option that does not use this technique. It is a work in which the student develops a system that is presumably compatible with the state of the art and then inserts some new characteristic into it to assess whether it has improved. Although it is not the most mature form of research, as it lacks a more universal benchmark, it is a valid form, except for item 3, which does not report anything specific about the work. However, for the method to be clearer, it would be necessary to specify what it means to add knowledge (the hypothesis) and show which tests would be carried out to test the validity or not of this hypothesis, in addition, of course, to a well-defined metric to compare the results. two approaches.

1. Use existing replication techniques and measure network and service performance.
2. Implement the proposed technique for replication in non-parallel services and measure network and service performance.

The research proposed here is very similar to the one immediately above. What would be the state of the art is implemented and compared with a version that has some new feature.

1. Bibliographic survey
2. Method creation
3. Adaptation or development of the software tool
4. Method application planning
5. Application of the method
6. Assessment
7. Conclusion

This presentation is particularly interesting because it fits almost any monograph as it is so generic. It practically consists of a template, from which the work schedule could be described. For this, it would be necessary to instantiate each of these steps in concrete activities related to the objectives of the work.

1. Development of a prototype of the four tools encompassing the concepts of modeling and workflow management in accordance with standardization [...].
2. Application of these tools in two hospitals affiliated to the project with the purpose of collecting statistical data for validation.

This proposal has the advantage, in relation to the previous ones, of explicitly mentioning the application of the technique being studied in real cases (hospitals).

However, data collection is mentioned, without making it very clear what type of data will be collected and what type of analysis will be carried out. Depending on the type of data to be collected, care must be taken, as they may not have statistical representation, as desired. An extreme example would be to consider that these are two hospitals specializing in cardiac surgery. If the majority of patients who are admitted there have cardiac treatment as their objective, this is not information that can be generalized to other hospitals. It is a fact only true in that reality, since there is a relationship between cause (the hospital is specialized in cardiac surgery) and effect (greater number of cardiac treatments in that hospital). Other, much more subtle relationships can occur. So the term "statistical" should be used very carefully.

Monograph writing

The writing of a monograph fundamentally depends on the existence of some content to be presented. The previous chapters presented ways to search for this content. This path begins with the choice of a problem, followed by the literature review, choice of an objective with a justified hypothesis, definition of a methodological procedure and its execution, for the collection of results that will be later analyzed and reported in the monograph.

10.1 Order of Presentation of Chapters

For those who read a monograph for the first time, it may seem that the work was written sequentially in the same way as it is presented. However, this is normally not the case.

The usual order of presentation of chapters in a monograph is as follows:

1. Summary
2. Introduction
3. Literature review
4. Development
5. conclusions
6. References

This order, mentioned earlier, is the one in which the work will be read by someone who is starting research in this area of knowledge. First, it is necessary to know the abstract to know what the work is about. The introduction presents objectives, limitations and methodological procedure of the work, in addition to placing it briefly in the state of the art. It will be necessary to read the literature review so that you know something about similar works, as well as the fundamental concepts for understanding the work itself, which is presented in the development chapter. Finally, the reader will observe the conclusions and, if he wants to learn more about the subject, he will consult the references listed at the end.

10.2 How Some Reviewers Read

It should be assumed that the examining board of a monograph is composed of specialists in the subject of the work, who already have sufficient knowledge of the main concepts and related works. These specialists will possibly read in a different order from the one presented in the previous section, initially seeking to obtain the most relevant information about the student's contribution, and then analyze the most trivial aspects of the work. The experts go straight to the heart of the matter, leaving the complements to evaluate in a second moment.

This varies widely, however, there will be reviewers who will simply read the work sequentially from start to finish, noting any inconsistencies and gaps as they progress through the text. How a reviewer reads a monograph depends on their personality and experience. However, a very interesting reading sequence, suggested by experts, could be defined as follows:

1. Summary
2. References
3. Introduction

4. Conclusion
5. Development
6. Literature review

The specialist initially reads the abstract to find out what the work is about. It checks if the abstract matches the title of the work. He expects the abstract to present the problem being addressed, a justification for the chosen hypothesis and, above all, a quick description of the obtained results or contributions. If any of these elements are not in the summary, the evaluator will likely already put a red checkmark here.

A work whose abstract does not clearly indicate the existence of relevant contributions may not be well evaluated. Therefore, it should be avoided that the abstract only presents information such as "This work presents a study on...", or "This work proposes a method for...".

It is necessary that the abstract presents some information such as "The main result obtained from this work is...". This result, it is assumed, must be relevant, in the sense that it was mentioned earlier, that is, it must correspond to some knowledge that was not available before the execution of the work and that was discovered during its elaboration. It will not be enough, for example, to write "The main result obtained from this work was the study of...", because, as has been said, the study is a personal objective of the student and not the objective itself of the research work. .

Subsequently, once the specialist has understood the abstract and known the real contribution of the work, he will verify if the alleged contribution was actually obtained. Initially, he will check the references cited by the student to see if the main works in the area are there. It will also check for recent articles in conferences and journals, as well as the relevance of those same conferences and journals.

Is it possible to fail a student based on the references cited in the work? At the master's and doctoral levels, yes. For example, consider a monograph (real case) on XML that presents as references 12 works, being three technical XML books and nine web pages that consist of technical XML manuals. In this case, there is no evidence of scientific work, but only of technical work. The student may even have made a very beautiful implementation of something with XML, but it will possibly have no scientific value if it is not based on works reported in events or periodicals.

If the references are adequate, the evaluator will observe the introductory chapter carefully. In this chapter he will understand in more detail the problem being solved, the technique used to solve it and how the results were validated. The evaluator will be especially attentive to the objectives of the work, including the specific objectives, which he will seek to identify clearly commented, one by one, in the conclusions.

When reading the conclusions, a good reviewer will scan the text for a conclusive comment on each of the objectives of the work, indicating evidence that the findings of the development chapter confirm the hypotheses or answer the research questions. The lack of this direct link between objectives and conclusions will certainly give rise to criticism.

After verifying the conclusions, the evaluator will turn his attention to the development chapter, in order to verify how the student reached those conclusions. The conclusions will all have to be consequences of evaluations made in the development chapter. It is not acceptable, for example, for a student to conclude that his system is easy to use if, in development, he only tested the system's efficiency, without checking its usability. To conclude something that was not verified throughout the work is called a "strong conclusion", being unacceptable in scientific works.

Having understood the student's real contribution, the evaluator will finally take a look at the literature review chapter to see if the main concepts were well presented and if the related works are adequately described and compared with the current work.

The way of reading described seems to go from the ends to the center of the monograph. The specialist focuses first on the critical points of the work and then reads the least problematic parts.

The order suggested in this book for writing the different chapters of a monograph differs from the previous two. You can write the monograph exactly in the order in which the chapters are presented. But this approach has some drawbacks, such as, for example, producing an unnecessarily long bibliographic review (because it does not know which concepts will actually be used in the text, everything is put on top of what has been read) and sometimes leaves the student tired in the process. time to write the most important thing: the conclusions. How many people have not handed their work to the advisor saying "It's done! All that is left is the conclusions"? However, the most important thing in a scientific work are the conclusions. The rest is just a convincing means of getting at them. Professor Doug Comer of Purdue University says:[1]

The easiest way to build a dissertation is inside-out. Begin by writing the chapters that describe your research [...]. Collect terms as they arise and keep a definition for each. Define each technical term, even if you use it in a conventional manner.[two]

It is recommended that you only start writing the final text after you have completed at least most of the research itself. Nothing prevents the writing of drafts, but these texts do not need to worry about formatting and organizing a finished text.

Then, when the student finishes the research and already has a very clear idea of what he did and what results he got, he will turn his drafts into a finished text. But in what order should he approach the writing of this text? Here's a suggestion:

1. Introduction
2. Development
3. conclusions
4. Literature review
5. References
6. Summary

It is recommended to start with the introduction because it is possibly the draft that will be closest to the final form at that moment. The introductory chapter is often a rewriting of the monograph proposal. The future tense is exchanged for the present tense, and the monograph has an objective, justification, hypotheses, etc., which were often the same as those of the research proposal. When some objective that existed at the beginning is not obtained for some reason, the ideal is to remove it from the objectives of the monograph, keeping only those that were obtained. However, it may be interesting to add a comment about this in the conclusions chapter, where in "future work" one can inform about the objective that was originally included in the list, but that was not achieved during the work.

Then the development must be written because the research, be it a case study, observation, experiment, survey, etc., will still be fresh to report. This is an important chapter, so it should be written very carefully.

Conclusions should be written soon afterwards. After finishing the development report, and having already revised the introductory chapter with its objectives clearly stated, the conclusion should be a consequence of what was reported in the development, as well as having a connection with each of the objectives, as already noted.

Only then is the bibliographic review written and the references listed. One should avoid placing in the bibliographic review all the works that may have been read, as this does not serve a clear objective. Instead, comparisons with correlated works and the main concepts used in the development chapter should be included. A concept that is not used in the development chapter, however interesting it may be, need not be in the theoretical foundation. The references will only mention the works actually cited. That's why it's important that these two sections are checked together.

Finally, the abstract is written, which, as the name says, summarizes the work. What should be said in this section of the work will be discussed later.

10.4 Title

The title of the work is the first means to catch the attention of a potential reader. A title should describe the main contribution of the work in a synthetic way. Some titles, because they are too generic, do not motivate reading. For example, "a study of neural networks". In order for it to be a good title, it would be better to say what kind of results this study produced. Another example of a non-motivating headline is "XYZ: A New Data Modeling Technique". Again, it would be more interesting if the title could clarify what kind of advantage this new technique would have over others. Just the fact that it's new doesn't guarantee it's interesting.

Here are some examples of good titles obtained from the Digital Library of the Brazilian Computer Society (SBC) a few years ago:

- *Formal Approaches to Ensuring the Safety of Space Software.*[3]
- *Automation of methods and techniques for functional testing of components.*
- *Electric Wheelchair Simulator for Rehabilitation of Persons with Motor Disability.*[4]
- *Comparative analysis of LBG and SOA dictionaries from the point of view of the computational complexity involved in the coding phase of vector quantization.*

10.5 Summary

The summary of a monograph is not, as some seem to think, a trailer for a movie, in which you begin to tell a story, but do not tell the end. The summary of a scientific work should give as much spoiler as possible, that is, it should tell the end of the story. The reader will want to know, first of all, what was the scientific result that this work arrived at. If he finds the result interesting in the abstract, he will want to read the rest to see how the author arrived at that result.

Hundreds of monographs in Computing are defended each year in Brazil alone. If we count other countries, we still have a large and growing amount of scientific material available. Expecting someone to read a monograph whose abstract reads "This paper presents a study of databases" is too much to expect. After all, that sentence says very little. What effectively could this "study" have generated in terms of new information that might interest someone working with databases? Why would a professional or researcher invest his time in reading this work, when thousands of others could possibly also be interesting?

It would be much more informative to have a summary that says something like: "This work demonstrates that the normal forms of existing databases are not sufficient to avoid a problem of data inconsistency identified here as...." If the reader is used to working with the normal shapes and thinks they explain what a good relational database should look like, he'll be curious to see what a weird case this is that isn't covered by the known shapes. Throughout the text, more details will be given, but the reader's attention has already been captured.

Therefore, the monograph summary is effectively the place to sell the fish. If the author cannot make a reader interested in the abstract, he will hardly be able to get him to read his monograph instead of others. Furthermore, indexing systems in abstract databases will also not identify the work properly.

One could argue that the abstract, usually less than one page, is too small a space to present a major contribution obtained in more than two years of work. But the problem is this: if the author cannot explain the contribution of his work on one page (abstract), there must be something very wrong with his work or his ability to be succinct.

One thing that is not done in the abstract is literature review. Unless it is vital for the understanding of the work, bibliographic citations should not be made in the abstract. It is unreasonable to waste valuable lines citing other people's work. This space is reserved for the author of the monograph to say what he came for and what he brought.

According to Professor Spencer Rugaber (1995), from Georgia Tech, the purpose of a monograph is the presentation of a thesis.[5]

So it makes sense to present this thesis as early as possible, that is, in the abstract. A thesis is defined as a statement that seeks to prove true. If a work at the master's or doctoral level cannot be defined from a thesis that can be expressed in one sentence, possibly something is wrong in the conception of the work.

10.6 Introduction

The introductory chapter will present the research topic and problem in more detail. Regarding the topic, a general description of the area and scope of the study is expected. However, very long introductions should be avoided, for example, starting in prehistory, in order to explain that the subject of the work is related to computer networks.

The introduction must contain the elements that have already been mentioned in the research project, that is, the general and specific objectives, expected results, limitations of the work, methodological procedures used and justification. In general, the introductory chapter is closed by a brief description of the other chapters of the work. In the case of methodological procedures, if their description is relatively long in relation to the other items, it can be presented in a separate chapter, usually between the introduction and the bibliographic review.

10.7 Bibliographic Review

The literature review can be understood as divided into two major parts:
- Theoretical foundation
- related works

The theoretical foundation must contain the concepts obtained in the literature and mentioned in the development and conclusions. Corresponding works will be state-of-the-art descriptions, that is, works that have published attempts to solve the same problem as the current work. This second part of the literature review can be obtained from a systematic literature review.

In the theoretical foundation it is important to be objective in the presentation, because the amount of texts to be consulted in most areas is very large. It is not recommended to make treatises or extensive digressions on works that are not directly related to the theme of the monograph. For example, if the work deals with the comparison between mutation techniques in genetic algorithms, it is not necessary to approach literature on robotics or neural networks, which, although they are topics directly linked to Artificial Intelligence, are collateral to the theme of the work.

The theoretical foundation should, rather, address the main concepts of the research area so that it can serve as a reference for eventual readers who are not exactly experts in the subject.

When it is necessary to mention concepts defined in more than one bibliographic source, it is suggested that the form of organization is to group the information by concept and not by author. For example, if authors A, B and C present concepts 1, 2 and 3, instead of citing concepts 1, 2 and 3 according to A, followed by concepts 1, 2 and 3 according to B and, finally, 1, 2 and 3 according to C, it is suggested that concept 1 be cited, according to A, B and C, if possible with some comparison or conclusion made by the author himself; later, the definitions for concept 2, according to A, B and C, and finally concept 3, according to A, B and C, are cited.

The related works section should describe research by each author individually and include a comparison with the current work, indicating what it is better (if quantitative) or at least different (if qualitative).

The comparison of the current work with related works can be done in two moments: in the bibliographic review and/or in the final considerations. At the end of the bibliographic review chapter, the research hypothesis can be compared with the related research hypotheses. We do not yet have effective data from the work because these data will only appear in the development chapter, but it is already possible to discuss the advantages and disadvantages of the different research hypotheses of each of the works or to advance results that will be presented in detail later.

The second time the comparison can be made is at the end of the document, usually at the end of the development chapter or in the concluding chapter or concluding remarks. At this point, the results of the work in question are already available, which can be compared with the results of other related works. It is, therefore, in this case, a much more objective and detailed comparison.

Rugaber (1995) states that the literature review section in general is dull and misused. This happens because the student, when writing, misses the opportunity to use the work of other authors to motivate his own study. Instead, time and space is often wasted making a tedious and unnecessary inventory of everything that has been read or a string of quotes from other authors that leads nowhere.

10.8 Development

The development chapter marks the beginning of the author's personal contribution to the work. Therefore, the development chapter should not be made a new bibliographic review. Preferably, all the concepts that will be needed in this chapter should have already been cited in the literature review chapter. If any comparison is made with related works in this chapter, only the objective comparison should be made here, the pure and simple presentation of the related works having already taken place in the previous chapter.

The development chapter should present the construction of the theory, experiments, model or proposal, of whatever nature. Concepts created by the author of the monograph should be described here and not in the literature review. Next, the author must work on the evidence that his hypothesis is true. Data, graphs, tests, formal evidence, case studies, interview transcripts or any other means deemed appropriate to prove your point, that is, to show that the hypothesis is true, will then be presented.

One should avoid turning the development chapter into a presentation of a computer system. If a system was developed, it was to serve some purpose of discovering new knowledge. The monograph should be about the knowledge generated, not about the system itself. Detailed presentations on software screens, including login screens, main menu, etc., are tedious and unnecessary in a scientific work. The following text, by Professor John W. Chinneck, sums it up:[6]

The purpose of your thesis is to clearly document an original contribution to knowledge. You may develop computer programs, prototypes, or other tools as a means of proving your points, but remember, the thesis is not about the tool, it is about the contribution to knowledge. Tools such as computer programs are fine and useful products, but you can't get an advanced degree just for the tool. You must use the tool to demonstrate that you have made an original contribution to knowledge; eg, through its use, or ideas it embodies.[7]

The conclusions chapter is, in general, the thorn in the student's side. Apparently everything has already been said about the work on the development chapter, so what to write in this final chapter?

The first tip is to observe the general and specific objectives of the work in the introductory chapter and place in the conclusions chapter a comment on how the presented development helped to reach each of these objectives, that is, how the research work allows to conclude that each one of the objectives has been achieved.

Another important point is to present not only the positive aspects of the work, but also the negative ones. No scientific work is expected to solve all the world's problems. On the contrary, the researcher is expected to be honest enough to clearly describe weaknesses and risks to the validity of his or her own work. The following maxim relentlessly follows the laws of logic: "If you are not the biggest critic of your own work, someone else will."

Another topic to be addressed in the conclusions chapter is lessons learned. The student spent two years or more studying a topic and experimenting with it. In addition to the work objectives, clearly stated and achieved, he must have learned a lot in the process. Perhaps this information can be useful to others. So, it is necessary to describe in the conclusions chapter what these lessons were learned during the work.

Other situations in which these lessons are thought to be applied can also be described. For example, when comparing the results of questionnaires applied in a company with the real situation observed in loco, a researcher noticed that, due to fear of retaliation by the superiors, most employees tried to present in the questionnaires a more beautiful situation than it really was. In this way, the researcher learned that, in this context, questionnaires are not reliable sources of information if there is no validation of the answers in the study environment. This lesson learned could be placed in the conclusions chapter.

The final chapter of a monograph must have at least three parts: conclusion, contributions and future work. At the conclusion, the student will make a concise reference to the problem examined and solved. According to John W. Chinneck, the conclusion itself will have the following format: "The problem described in section x was solved as demonstrated in sections y and z, in which an algorithm/method/approach, etc. was developed. to deal with the aforementioned situations."[8]

Also according to Chinneck, the summary of contributions, which would follow, should be organized in descending order of importance, for example:

- A much faster algorithm was developed for large Zylon problems.
- The use of the Grooty mechanism for Zylon calculations was demonstrated for the first time.

Published articles and research reports are not contributions, in this sense of the word, but research reports. Eventually, they may be cited here, or presented as appendices at the end of the work. Taking advantage of the mention: appendices are materials produced by the author of the monograph that are placed at the end for consultation so as not to interfere with the flow of reading the work. Attachments are materials produced by other sources that are added to the monograph for consultation. For example, a student who is doing a project on Informatics and Law may present as annexes a set of laws and jurisprudence relevant to the work for the reader to consult. Another example would be attaching tables queried in computer systems powered by third parties. Care must be taken, however, not to attach copyrighted material to the monograph. To find out which materials may or may not be used in Brazil, you can consult the Copyright Law, or Law 9,610 of February 19, 1998.

Finally, future works are the contribution that the student leaves so that others can continue their research. Future work should also address future contributions to knowledge with more emphasis than future contributions to tools, prototypes, etc., that may eventually be developed.

It is always expected that a monograph is not only the end of a research, but also the beginning of a journey.

Thus, the final section of conclusions is usually dedicated to leaving readers with ideas of research opportunities that the author came across in the course of his work, but that he did not have the time or opportunity to pursue.

In this section tips on future research work are expected, not future technical work. For example, the reader will have little interest in knowing that the author intends to implement the system in Java in the future, since the current version is in C. This is just a technical issue. The reader will want to know which situations have not been tested with the current tool that could be relevant to understanding their behavior. This would be relevant future research work.

10.10 Bibliographic References

It is not the purpose of this book to present bibliographic citation standards, as they are available in any self-respecting library. As there are different citation standards, it is suggested to follow the norms established by the course, journal or event in which the work will be published.

10.11 Form of Scientific Text

Scientific text must communicate a research idea and its results. This, of course, is a semantic issue. But there are a number of small vices that many students have that, because they are so common, are mentioned here so they can be avoided.

This section is not intended to teach you how to write correct Portuguese or how to format monographic works or articles. The objective is to present and discuss frequent mistakes made by Computer Science students in their work, which can be easily minimized.

First, a monograph should avoid, whenever possible, the use of adverbs. Strange, no? The adverb is a word that modifies a verb and is very common in the Portuguese language. However, the use of the adverb in the scientific text often spoils a sentence that, without it, could be much better. Although the adverb can be very useful for emphasizing ideas, in scientific text the use of the adverb should be minimized as it can unnecessarily reinforce certain statements. For example, saying that "experience demonstrates that the approaches are equivalent" is one thing, but saying "experience definitely demonstrates that the approaches are equivalent" gives an air of arrogance to the text, which is not necessary for the sentence in question. . You can see that the two sentences have the same meaning, but the first one sounds much better than the second.

Something to be avoided in a scientific text is also jokes, jokes or irony. Eventually, scientific journals even publish texts with this type of resource, but in these cases, in general, the author is some big shot in the area. Anyone who is not the Pope should not risk using these resources in the scientific text. It would be like going to your boyfriend's parents' house for the first time and deciding to unleash your entire repertoire of jokes. Do you have a chance of succeeding?

In a scientific text, the author is not expected to use value judgment on topics that cannot be evaluated as bad or good in a Manichean way. To say, for example, that object orientation is good while structured programming is bad for software development is a matter of opinion. Instead of saying that something is good, one should try to emphasize one of the qualities that is thought to be good. Instead of saying something is bad, an explanation based on verifiable facts should be presented about the defects that are thought to be a problem.

One should never say that something is "perfect" because in nature nothing is.

Instead of writing expressions like "nowadays" and "currently", it is better to use the current year. This is because it is not known, a priori, when the text will be read. So, instead of writing "currently", you can write "in 2019". In this way, the sentence will be more precise and will give a better scientific basis to any other information that is presented next.

Statements like "a new approach", "a different technique", etc. must be avoided. Any approach being proposed will be new and different from others; otherwise, it would not be the subject of a monograph. It wouldn't make sense to propose something that is old or the same as what already exists, would it? So, one should avoid qualifying the work as new and different, as this is already what everyone expects. It is better to just say, after all, what the job is and how it is different or better than the previous ones.

Using words like "obviously" or "clearly" can insult the reader, as the author claims to be saying something that is obvious. If it's obvious it doesn't have to be said, if it's not obvious then it shouldn't be said. So obviously one should avoid using that term.[10]

Whenever the text uses the expression "in fact" it can give the impression that what was written before was a lie. So actually this is not a good choice.[11]

It is usual, in the dissertation text, that the author does not make a personal narrative such as "I saw", "I tested", "I discovered", etc. Instead, it is usually written "was seen", "has been tested", "has been discovered", etc. But this is a custom more observed in Brazil and some other countries. Texts published internationally more frequently present sentences written in the first person singular or, when they are texts with several authors, in the first person plural.

When one of the pronouns "all", "many", "some" or "none" is used, one must be sure that there is evidence or proof that the statement can actually be qualified as such. It cannot be said in a scientific text, for example, that "many students have problems with the monograph", without there having been a study, observation or measurement about it. Another possibility is to use a quote. Saying "according to So-and-so (2019), most students have problems with the monograph" is correct, because it passes the problem of proving the claim to the author of the quoted text. However, in this case, it is still necessary to verify that the reference is a reliable and good quality work.

Other recommendations are to use the active voice instead of the passive, write in the present tense and put negations at the beginning of the sentence. These style recommendations help make the text easier to understand.

Thus, "the study demonstrates the validity of the hypothesis" (active voice) should be preferred over "the validity of the hypothesis was demonstrated by the study" (passive voice). Some text editors already make this a default style correction suggestion.

It would be difficult to read a long sentence in which a series of things is stated and at the end an expression is used to indicate that everything that was being said is false. If the goal is to deny something, then it is preferable to start by denying it. This will make the text easier to understand. In any case, it is always preferable to use affirmative sentences when possible. Instead of saying, "confirmation of the experiment carried out over three months by the teams did not happen" (denial at the end), it is preferable to say "the confirmation of the experiment carried out over three months by the teams did not happen".

Another example of denial at the end comes from the book The Hitchhiker's Guide to the Galaxy (Adams, 2004) with the phrase "An expression of deep worry and concern failed to cross either of Zaphod's faces".[12]It's an ironic phrase, because the book is in the humorous style, but it illustrates well the strangeness caused by reading a phrase that affirms things and in the end denies everything.

Chinneck presents some interesting tips for the text:

- Always keep the reader's background in mind. One must know what comprehension capacity the target reader of the text will have. The text must be informative enough for that target reader. Do not go into too much detail on concepts that would be trivial and do not fail to explain concepts that are not likely to be known to the target reader.
- Don't make the reader have to work hard. Knowing what the student's obligations are in the text (to make the research problem clear, to show that it had not yet been

solved, to show that the problem was worth solving and to show that the student actually solved the problem), one must leave the text as accessible as possible. The more difficult it is for reviewers to find answers to key questions about the paper, the worse their impression of the text and the more likely they are to demand major changes to the final text.

- Write in such a way that it is impossible to be clearer. You should write each sentence very carefully, check if it makes sense and if it presents any useful information clearly. It must be verified that each term used in each sentence has already been properly explained at the level of understanding of the target reader and that all possible ambiguities have been eliminated.
- Remember that the monograph is not a story. It is not a chronology of the things the student has tried to do, but a formal document that presents the results of a survey.
-

One more suggestion could be added: write the sentences as short as possible. For example, one can say "roses are considered to have the property of being seen as red". But one can also say much the same thing with the phrase "roses are red".

Professor Mirella M. Moro from the Federal University of Minas Gerais (UFMG) presents the seven deadly sins of the scientific text:[13]

- *long sentences*(full of commas or not). Whenever very long sentences with several coordinated sentences are detected, one should try to divide them into smaller sentences, using dots for this. But care must be taken so that each sentence read individually makes sense, having subject, verb and object, when applicable.
- *Spelling errors*. Nothing disqualifies an author more than spelling errors, that is, poorly written words. Good

content can even go unnoticed if the author makes mistakes of this kind.

- *literal translation and*"imbromation". An author who is not fluent in English should seek the help of a translator and, in most cases, also a professional proofreader in that language.
- *Unreadable images/tables*. Are very small or blurry letters used to communicate something? Captions that, in color, are perfect, but when printed in black and white are indistinguishable should also be reviewed and avoided.
- *grammatical errors*(parallelism, agreement, conjugation, crasis). Concordance errors end up being very common because of bad revisions of the text. Sometimes you change the subject of a sentence from masculine to feminine or from singular to plural and leave the verb or complements as they were. For example, the original sentence looked like this: "The method was tested..." A review changed the term "method" to "steps" and the final text looked like this: "The steps were tested [sic]...." The error appears only on the last word.
- *Literal copy*. If there is a literal copy of other texts without using quotation marks and citing the source, plagiarism is incurred. However, even with citation, the use of literal copying should be minimized. This type of expedient should only be used when it is impossible to be clearer than the literal author.
- *Blah blah blah*(fill sausage). How many pages should a monograph have? Sometimes, students think that their work is too short and decide to fill pages with texts that don't say anything just to give more sense of volume.

- *Use automatic proofing tools*. Although nothing replaces careful reading by the author, his advisor and eventually by third parties as well, the use of automatic reviewers helps to eliminate errors that could go unnoticed.

- *Divide paragraphs carefully.* Each paragraph must present a central idea that can be introduced and commented on in the same paragraph. When a new idea is introduced, a new paragraph is usually started. Both too long and too short paragraphs should be avoided.

- *A section or chapter must consist of more than one paragraph.* If a section contains only one paragraph, then it shouldn't be a section, but a paragraph within some other section. Also, sections and chapters cannot be divided into a single section. For example, if chapter 1 has section 1.1, then there must be at least 1.2. Otherwise, consider keeping Chapter 1 without any sections.

- *Each sentence must have a subject and a verb.* Only the titles of sections, figures and tables can be composed of sentences without a verb (eg "Final tests"). Sentences included in the text must always have at least one verb. On the other hand, the text of a section cannot be a continuation of the section title. For example, it would be wrong to title a section "3.2.1. Final tests" and start the first paragraph of the section with "They were carried out satisfactorily". The correct thing would be to start the paragraph with a sentence with subject and verb that can be read independently of the section title, in this case: "The final tests were carried out to our satisfaction." Also, it is a style mistake to create a section (eg "3.2.1 Examples of algorithms") and fill it with just a list of items. The section always starts with text. Item lists can be part of the section, but never its entirety.

- *clarified acronyms.* Whenever an acronym is used for the first time, it must be defined in full. Even if it appears in the list of abbreviations at the beginning of the monograph, it must still be presented in full in the text the first time it is used. This is even true for very famous acronyms in certain areas (eg XP [eXtreme Programming] or RUP [Rational Unified Process] in the case of software engineering).

Hexsel (2004) adds a few more suggestions:

- Highlight terms using italics and not bold, as the former has a nicer effect than the latter.
- Use flat graphics, which are lighter than pseudo-three-dimensional ones (Figure 10.1).
- Avoid anglicisms whenever possible, for example using "link" or "link" instead of "link" or "performance" instead of "performance".
- Insert the bibliographic references so that they do not interfere with the flow of the text,

    Given the habit of working with programming languages, computer students sometimes forget how to properly use punctuation marks. In a text, you never put a space before the punctuation mark, but you always put a space after the punctuation mark if there is a word after it. See examples and counterexamples below.
- This is a sentence. The period of the previous sentence should have a space after it.
- This is a sentence. The period of the previous sentence has a space before it should not exist.
- This is a sentence. The end point is well placed.

    In the case of parentheses, square brackets and braces, there should never be a space inside these symbols. If outside there is a word, space is used. However, if after closing parenthesis or similar there is a punctuation mark, no space is used. Examples below:
- This text (correctly formatted) is in parentheses.
- This other one (poorly formatted) was left with the open parenthesis pasted on the previous word.

- This one (badly formatted) has an extra space after the opening parenthesis.
- Finally (well formatted), this one suppresses the space after the closing parenthesis because of the comma.

When in doubt, the student should always try to read a lot and see how the texts are formatted and not invent new formats, nor follow the usual standards of programming languages, as these apply to programs, not texts.

A final aspect that is a very common error in Computing monographs is the inappropriate use of capital letters at the beginning of words. In general, there are two rules that must be observed. Firstly, titles of chapters or sections of text usually do not have a punctuation mark at the end, but nouns, adjectives and most verbs must start in capital letters. Examples follow:

- *Title of Work with Capital Letters Correctly Used.*
- *Title of Work with Endpoint That Shouldn't Exist.*

A title will only have final punctuation if it is a question mark or exclamation mark. For example:

- *How to make a correct title?*

Now, in relation to the use of capital letters in the text in general, it is used only at the beginning of sentences (new paragraph or after a period) or in the case of proper nouns. It is wrong to capitalize randomly, as many students do. See these examples:

- The System that was developed... ("system" is not a proper name).
- This Dissertation was written... ("Dissertation" is not a proper name).
- During the Inaugural Class it was presented... ("inaugural class" is not a proper name).

These are style rules that, in general, do not affect the content of a work, but help to make it more readable.

More rules can be found in the Portuguese Orthographic Agreement of 1990 in its Base XIX.[14]

---

[7]Translation: "The aim of your thesis is to clearly document an original contribution to knowledge. You can develop computer programs, prototypes or other tools as a means of proving your points, but remember, the thesis is not about the tool, it is about the contribution to knowledge. Tools such as computer programs are cool and useful products, but you can't get an advanced academic degree just for the tool. You must use the tool to demonstrate that you have made an original contribution to knowledge.

Scientific article

The scientific article is the academically recognized form of dissemination of a research work. At the master's level, and especially at the doctoral level, it is expected, and in some cases is required, the publication of an article in a conference or journal of good quality. This chapter presents some tips on writing articles and ends with comments on the Brazilian system for evaluating the quality of publication vehicles, Qualis, defined by Capes (Coordination for the Improvement of Higher Education Personnel), linked to the Ministry of Education.

All recommendations regarding the text of the monograph are also valid for scientific articles. There is also the recommendation that the article should be much more succinct than the monograph. So clarity and objectivity are much more critical in an article than in a monograph.

11.1 Authors

Unlike the monograph, which is an individual work, the scientific article will often be a collaborative work. In the case of the monograph, the author is the student and the advisor is not considered a co-author. But if the monograph gives rise to one or more scientific articles, it is natural for the supervisor to be a co-author, although, normally, he appears in second place. Other co-authors may be invited to participate in the writing of the article, if necessary.

There is no consensus on the order in which authors should appear in the article. In some cases, it is recommended, for simplicity, to use alphabetical order. However, the first author of an article is often considered the most important. And using alphabetical order can create some confusion. It can be difficult, in the case of cooperative work between researchers or institutions, to reach a conclusion about who is the main author. But, in the case of articles inspired by monographs, this decision is much simpler:

-
- Secondly, the supervisor's name should appear, as he or she also has great responsibility for the original work, as well as for its final review.
- Thirdly, co-advisors, colleagues or other researchers who have somehow contributed to the text may appear, if any.

The usual thing is that only people who effectively participated in the writing of the text are considered co-authors, although sometimes people who have helped in the collection of data or in the implementation of the prototypes that gave rise to the work are also mentioned. A very large list of co-authors is generally not recommended, because it can give the impression that you are artificially trying to improve someone's CV. But eventually this may be the case, especially when it comes to work arising from inter-institutional cooperation.

11.2 Motivation to Write

You shouldn't write an article if you don't know yet what you're going to say. It sounds like common sense, but sometimes students start a job that way.

First, the candidate for author should think of a sentence that summarizes the contribution of the article and then develop that sentence by presenting the background, detail and consequences of this idea. If you can't think of a sentence that summarizes the article, the author is in trouble. It might be interesting to stop and think a little more, or even better develop the research, organize ideas, look for the advisor and then try again.

An article is the communication of an idea. One must not speak for the sake of speaking. One should not write aimlessly or waste precious lines with irrelevant or disconnected information.

A scientific article is usually a short text, with eight to twelve pages. Rarely will an article be longer than sixteen pages. So, the article cannot and should not be a treaty about an area of knowledge, but the objective and precise transcription of a research idea, the development that validated it and its consequences in the world.

The article should not be a complete presentation of a tool, prototype, method or process. For this, you can write a manual or technical report with as many pages as you want. The article must emphasize the concrete result obtained in the research. It is also important to show the reader how the author arrived at this result and, after all, what the real problem is that the result solves.

For a better understanding of the subject, the reader should receive, at the beginning of the article, a summary of the main concepts, only those essential to understand the results. It is noted that establishing the concepts necessary for understanding the article often depends on the type of publication vehicle. For example, to write an article about neural networks applied to stock market forecasting systems and publish it in a Computing event, it is not necessary to define what neural networks are, it is enough to mention which model was used, why it was chosen and put a bibliographic citation. On the other hand, the economics concepts used will possibly have to be explained in more detail so that a computer reader can understand the research. On the other hand, if the publication takes place in an Economy event, the opposite happens. One should explain in more detail what a neural network is and how it works, and one can have more parsimony in relation to the concepts of Economics.

Snyder (1991) proposes that the author of an article ask himself a few questions before submitting the article to an event. The first of these questions is: "Why am I writing this article?". If the answer is "To document what I have been doing for the past two years", the author is in serious danger of having his work rejected. Few people will be interested in knowing what someone has done in the last two years. If the goal is to document these activities, the author should write a research report, not an article.

Another wrong answer would be, "To improve my resume." This could even be the initial motivation for someone to write an article, but it will hardly motivate others to accept the text for publication. Then another answer must be sought.

The correct answer to the question would be along the lines of "Communicate an idea to someone". So, still according to Snyder, the following questions would be: "What is my article trying to communicate?" and "What is the target audience of my article?". If the author cannot categorically answer these two questions, there is a high chance that it is a weak article.

Another issue is that a focused article is more likely to be good than a scattered article. It is better to take an idea and work it out clearly in the article than to skim over a large set of ideas that the author has had throughout his life. In the case of multiple ideas, it is better to write multiple articles.

After knowing clearly what the article is communicating, the author must still ask himself if it is worth presenting this communication, that is, is he really communicating a new idea or is it just a new way of presenting an old idea that has already is it very well known? Is it a relevant idea or is it trivial? Is it just conjecture or information based on solid evidence?

11.3 Related Works

Not only an article, but also the final monograph, must mention related works. Excuses such as "No one has ever done anything like it" (because "similar" is a diffuse and very flexible term) or "I haven't found anything in the bibliography about it" (the reader will always think that not enough search has been done) are not accepted. A smart student will avoid falling into this trap!

But what to do if nothing is actually found? For example, if someone is researching the applications of neural networks in the stock market and no matter how hard they look, they can't find any other work on this subject, how to escape this trap?

In doing so, the reader is more relaxed. No one can be blamed for not having found an article on the subject that was eventually published in an obscure local event in some foreign language other than English, for no one is able to know everything, right? But the student will be well supported if this article exists and if an evaluator mentions it, as he delimited his bibliographic review by carrying out a systematic mapping. If that work in a language spoken by few is really good, why wasn't it submitted to the good publishing vehicles recognized by the community and available in the databases in English?

11.4 Article Contribution

Regarding the contribution of the article, one can recommend:

- Don't be modest!
- Don't overdo it!

For Plato (2006), vices are in extremes, and virtue, in balance. So, the author must be realistic about the results and contribution of his article.

The author must convince the review committee that his results are correct. They should not be expected to simply believe in ideas or sympathize with them. They need to be convinced. The review committee will critically read the article, looking for lapses that could invalidate the work. To be published, the work must pass this sieve. So a critical conviction is needed. Evidence, evidence and examples should be presented that might help.

Finally, the contribution of the article must be clear from the abstract or abstract. It cannot be left to the end. The results should be presented at the beginning of the article to interest the reader. Then the author can go on explaining how he got to them.

11.5 Types of Articles

There are several types or styles of articles, each of which has its own characteristics and its own publishing vehicles. This section highlights a few.

A theoretical paper basically presents a set of definitions, known as a "theory", and then goes on to prove logical properties of that set. Examples of proof techniques used in this type of article are induction (mathematical or structural) and reduction to absurdity.

In a theoretical paper, each claim needs to be put carefully, and all need to be substantiated. A statement can be substantiated by means of a bibliographic reference, logical proof, direct observation report, or even as a hypothesis or definition.

However, there is no point in just taking a theoretical approach to an issue. It is necessary to show what the real problem is that this theory solves. So there's no point in creating a pretty theory that serves no purpose. Even a theoretical paper must have some kind of consequence in the world.

11.5.2 Experience Report

An experience report tells an informative story about an experiment and its observations. This account should show how the observed situation reflects more general situations. That is, the experience report should, whenever possible, not focus on the specific instance being observed, but present the possible generalization of the observations to other situations.

Avoid going into irrelevant details about the experiment. Only the information necessary to understand or validate the report should be incorporated.

The report should focus on the ideas, not the experiment itself. That is, the experience report is not a narrative about all the steps that the author took on the path of observation, but a structuring of the ideas learned during the observation. This structuring, then, will rarely be presented in a temporal narrative form, but in an essay form, organized by concepts and their implications.

11.5.3 Article on Methods

Articles on methods are especially common in Computer Science. A good method article cannot simply be a method presentation. It should focus on the advantages that the presented method has over others previously proposed for the same or similar problems.

A method article should have a clear informational purpose, that is, the new method should have a focal point. The article should list the advantages of the new method over previous approaches. So, here, the bibliographic comparison is fundamental for the acceptance of the article.

It is recommended that an article on methods allows the application of the method in a real project. When this is not possible, reference to a more complete text may help. Also, as the article must contain a comparison with pre-existing methods, it must make it very clear which metric is used for the comparison. A subjective comparison will be of little value, especially if the author does not make it clear where the results came from. For example, a table of characteristics, in which several methods are compared, evaluating each one with the value "meets", "does not meet" or "meets partially", will not have much value, unless the author makes it very clear how these assessments were obtained so that they can be repeated by independent observers.

The article must be more than a method presentation with explanation. The important thing is not to list the operating procedures of the new method, but to present the ideas that the new method embodies.

Furthermore, the article must be balanced. New approaches are often not the universal panacea. If the new method has advantages, it will possibly also have limitations, which should be described and analyzed in the article.

11.6 Publication Vehicles

Research results can be published in a number of vehicles recognized by the scientific community. The greater the impact of the vehicle, that is, the number of people it effectively reaches, the greater the relative difficulty of managing to publish an article there.

So, depending on the actual contribution and innovation of the work, different publishing vehicles should be chosen. The student should not be discouraged if his first attempt at publication is unsuccessful. Usually, consistent critical evaluations of the work are delivered explaining the reasons for the refusal. These assessments can and should be used as a stimulus and a guide to produce an improved version of the article for publication elsewhere.

There are vehicles that are very specific to each area, such as the Brazilian Symposium on Software Quality or the IEEE Transactions on Software Engineering. But they are not the only vehicles in which you can publish. There are more general journals and events that, in general, accept articles from all areas of Computing; for example, SEMISH (Integrated Software and Hardware Seminar), which takes place together with the Brazilian Computer Society Congress, and the Communications of ACM journal. Both are considered good vehicles.

Regarding the style of the vehicle, the following distinctions can be made:

- *periodicals*: They are considered the most important publication by all areas of science. The best articles are usually destined for the most recognized journals within each area. Computer Science around the world, however, has few journals when compared to other areas of knowledge. In Brazil, quality journals in Computer Science are rare.

- *conferences*: Computer Science privileges publication in conferences, which often creates problems in relation to evaluation related to other areas, such as Physics and Chemistry, whose researchers publish almost exclusively in journals. Although not as valued as journals in other areas, conferences in Computing can have a very relevant relative weight in the scientific production of a researcher.

- *workshops*and seminars: These are usually satellite events of larger conferences. As they are usually very restricted in terms of thematic scope and number of participants, they are considered less impactful publications, although some workshops have established themselves as good conferences throughout a consistent history of good editions.

- *Books and book chapters*: Although highly valued, books and book chapters are publications that usually do not result from theses and monographs (with few exceptions), since, in general, the objective of this type of publication is to present didactic content for understanding by a well-educated public. broader than the set of researchers in a given area of science.

There is a fundamental difference in the style of the event and journal review process. As the events take place on a predetermined date, publications are usually submitted by a certain deadline (deadline) and then evaluated by a program committee. This is normally a competitive process in which the best articles are accepted for publication, with a few suggestions for text modification. Most events, especially the more highly regarded ones, will accept a relatively small percentage of submitted papers. So, in the case of submitting an article to an event, the author will only have one chance to publish. The article must be ready and able to compete with other articles. If it is among the best, it will be published; otherwise, it will be rejected.

The review process in journals takes place in a different way. Except in the case of special thematic issues, the periodicals work on a continuous basis, that is, there is no deadline. Thus, an article eventually accepted in the journal enters a queue and will be published when its turn comes. The review process, then, can be much more interactive than in the case of events.

A submitted article will be reviewed by the editorial committee and, possibly, various suggestions will be made to the text before it can be accepted for publication. There may even be several rounds of text evaluation, in which reviewers request changes, and authors incorporate them into the text, if possible. This interactive process of reviewing a text can even take years, in some cases, but seeks to ensure that the final material will be suitable for the journal's readership, according to the criteria of the editorial committee.

It should also be borne in mind that the review process in journals is much more detailed than in conferences. In the case of conferences, reviewers work with deadlines and are sometimes given a large burden of evaluation to do, thus being more prone to making evaluation errors. In the case of journals, the review takes longer and is therefore much more detailed.

Regarding books, care must be taken, especially after the publication of the monograph, as the phenomenon of predatory publishers has grown, offering newly graduated students the possibility of transforming their monograph into a book, edited and sold by the publisher. Normally, the editorial process is simply one of diagramming, and the student will incur high expenses to see their work published and then sold at very high prices, which discourages the effective dissemination of the material. In the end, the student will be able to purchase the rest of the copies from the publisher at a discount, but still expensive, to distribute among relatives and friends. It should be emphasized that the business of these publishers consists more in profiting from the author than in carrying out the dissemination of scientific work.

There are, however, more serious publishers and these usually make a contract with the candidate author so that the publisher is responsible for all the costs of producing the book, and the author is only responsible for submitting the original manuscript to the editorial board. After the book is published and commercialized, the author will receive royalties periodically, according to the contract signed with the publisher.

In addition to the type of publication, the scope must also be considered. All the different vehicles have an estimated range, which can be:

- *International*: vehicles published in English that are distributed or have the participation of authors from several countries, with no predominance of any nation, such as, for example, most IFIP, ACM and IEEE journals and conferences.
- *National*: it is not just the vehicles published in Brazil, as one might think. There are national journals and conferences published in other countries. A national vehicle is one that is published in a language other than English or that, although published in English, has participants predominantly from a single country or

region, for example, the Latin American Informatics Conference (CLEI) and most of the SBC symposia.

- *Regional*: are vehicles that cover only a fraction of a country, for example, a Brazilian state and/or geographic region. Examples of this type of vehicle are the proceedings of the Regional School of Databases and the Santa Catarina Seminar on Medical Images.
- *Local*: are vehicles published by a single university or college. In general, they have a local or small-scale review committee, and most authors of articles belong to the institution itself. For example, the X University Informatics Week.

There are, then, combinations between the different types of publication and their scope, such as, for example, international journal or regional event, etc. The computer science area document at Capes distinguishes the following types: international journal (PI), national journal (PN), international conference (CI), national conference (CN), national scientific book (LCN), national textbook (LDN), international scientific book (LCI), international textbook (LDI), national book chapter (CLN) and international book chapter (CLI).

Attention should be paid to the following: some conferences publish their proceedings as books, with ISBN included. There is no consensus in the community on whether this characterizes a book publication or a conference publication. However, logically, only the literary work that was proposed and built for that purpose should be considered a book. A book has a sequential and logical structure, which conferences do not usually have, because they publish the best articles. But these are submitted independently by their authors, based on the research work they have carried out, without a predetermined logical sequence.

The computer age, however, has facilitated the creation of publications so much that the clear boundaries that once existed between different types of publications may no longer exist in the future.

11.7 *Qualis*

The Coordination for the Improvement of Higher Education Personnel (Capes), an agency of the Ministry of Education of Brazil, publishes a list of vehicles used to disseminate the intellectual production of stricto sensu graduate programs (masters and doctorate), classified according to their relative impact by assessment area. This list, which represents the journal evaluation system, Qualis, is used by Capes to support the evaluation process of the National Postgraduate System.

Qualis, which until 2019 was organized by knowledge area, became unique for all areas, that is, each journal has a unique concept in the Qualis list. Journals are vehicles with a recognized editorial body, with peer review (ad hoc reviewers), equipped with ISSN and appearing in internationally recognized databases. Bibliometric indicators related to these databases are Scopus (CiteScore), Web of Science (impact factor) and Google Scholar (H5 index).

Journals are thus classified into nine levels: A1, A2, A3, A4, B1, B2, B3, B4 and C, with A1 being the highest level, indicating a journal of excellence and C the lowest level, indicating that this is a journal that does not comply with good editorial practices, such as peer review.

Academic Ethics

A point to always be mentioned when talking about academic ethics is the issue of plagiarism. Under no circumstances can texts written by another person be used, even in a work of an eminently school nature, without putting the quoted text in quotation marks and mentioning the reference source. Using someone else's work as if it were your own is considered a crime of plagiarism under Brazilian law.

Even translations should be avoided. If it is the case of mentioning any text in another language, it is recommended that it be kept in the original in quotation marks and with the cited source. Optionally, a translation can be added in a footnote. If the source of reference is the translated work, it can be cited according to the language in which it was translated (in this case, Portuguese), but if the translation is done by the author of the work, it is recommended to keep the original and use the footnote for the translation, as it is not an official translation and therefore the meaning of the translation cannot be attributed to the author of the original text.

Plagiarism is the misappropriation of other people's ideas or texts. The practice of copying someone else's work was common and accepted among ancient scribes and Renaissance and Baroque musicians, but over time and with the consolidation of the right to property and its exploitation, plagiarism acquired the status of an unethical procedure. . However, it always happened. In the age of the internet, it's never been easier to copy someone else's work, but it's also never been easier to detect those copies.

Regardless of the issue of commercial exploitation of copyright, plagiarism, in the academic environment, is extremely harmful if not detected, because the plagiarist presents a result that is not of its authorship and receives a title that it does not deserve. In this condition, he himself can be harmed, by not mastering knowledge that would be necessary to exercise his profession or, worse still, if he exercises his profession, he will harm others, by presenting inadequate solutions, according to his own incompetence.

There are at least two forms of plagiarism: the literal copying of texts by other people, constituting in whole or in part a work that should belong to the author, and the copying of ideas, in which the author, despite not repeating the words as they were written, presents the same ideas, in the same logical sequence, as if they were your own.

The use of third-party ideas is not considered plagiarism as long as the source is clearly identified. In the case of literal copies, they must appear in quotation marks.

It is said that, once, a doctoral student plagiarized a thesis, copying the full text of another author and changing only the name of the original author to his own name (actual case). During the defense, one of the panel members, the external guest, lavishly praised the work for several minutes. In the end he added, "But you can't get a doctorate with that thesis, because that work is mine." The plagiarist was so careless that he didn't even look at the name of the person who was plagiarizing and ended up inviting that person to the bank.

12.1 Background

Until the invention of the printing press, written works were reproduced by professional scribes and copyists. At that time, only these copy professionals were paid for their work. The author was only credited with the work (but sometimes not even that).

With the invention of the printing press, in the 15th century, copying texts became a mass activity and, for this reason, raised the question of legal protection of the author's work. Not only the issue of protecting the right to the heritage of the work, but also the protection of its integrity.

At first, censorship went hand in hand with copyright protection. In 1662, for example, in England, the Licensing Act forbade the printing of any book that had not been previously authorized. The Copyright Act of 1709, on the other hand, protected the intellectual and patrimonial property of printed works for up to 21 years.

In France, after the Revolution of 1789, Enlightenment values began to prevail and, with that, the primacy of the author over the intellectual work. Copyright protection became valid for the life of the author, including passed on to his legal heirs.

In Brazil, the first mention of copyright protection appeared in 1827, in the law that created legal courses. In 1830, the matter was regulated through the enactment of the criminal law code.

12.2 Copyright Protection

Brazil has one of the strongest copyright laws in the world. In the United States, for example, copyright protection depends on registration. In Brazil, registration is not a precondition for copyright protection. Proof of authorship is sufficient. You can, for example, seal the literary or technical work in a mail envelope and send it to yourself or a person you trust. This envelope should not be opened except in court. The postmark is proof of the date of production, or at least shows that on the date of shipment the production was with the person in question. Thus, in the case of a lawsuit for plagiarism, the author can prove that the text was with him on a certain date. If this date is before the production considered plagiarism, a good part of the process will have been resolved in favor of the author.

In undergraduate courses and graduate programs, there is great concern about plagiarism. In particular, because it has never been so easy to copy texts using the internet. On the other hand, too, it has never been easier to detect copies. Sophisticated tools are not even needed for this. All you need is a search engine and a copy of the monograph. Three or four words are chosen at random at any point in the monograph and searched on the search engine. The occurrence of these words together in a text is hardly coincidental. With this feature, it is possible to discover the vast majority of cases of plagiarism.

Texts translated from other languages into Portuguese are more difficult to detect, but not so much. Usually, the writing style itself allows us to perceive that a text is a translation and not a text originally written in Portuguese. For example, Brazilians rarely use the word "eventually" or "pronece" in scientific texts when writing in Portuguese, but translate these words literally from texts in English, where they are more common (in this case, respectively, " eventually" and "provides").

It is believed that much of academic plagiarism occurred because students were not correctly oriented as to what could and could not be copied. So, so that there is no doubt, here is the answer: nothing can be copied, unless it is placed in quotation marks and with the citation of the bibliographic source. Even so, one should act with parsimony, as citations cannot predominate in a scientific work. The author's contribution is required.

Once, a specialization student delivered a 20-page monograph (actual case). On the front page, he wrote something like "I read an interesting article on the internet the other day". Then he would unquote and include said article literally in the monograph. Twenty pages later, after closing quotation marks, he concluded by saying: "That's why I found the article so interesting." The student failed. He questioned saying that since he had put the text in quotation marks and cited the source, it was not plagiarism. But he failed anyway, because apart from what was in quotation marks, there was practically nothing left of his work. Thus, the work was considered insufficient to obtain the title.

12.3 The Brazilian Law

It is interesting to know what Brazilian law says. The main reference, in the case of plagiarism, is Law 9,610, of February 19, 1998. This law changes, updates and consolidates the legislation on copyright.

A frequent question in the area of Computing is whether the government, by subsidizing a project, becomes the copyright holder of it. For example, if the student receives a grant from Capes or CNPq to write his monograph, do these bodies have any rights over the monograph and its products? The law is clear in its art. 6th:

The works that they simply subsidize will not be the domain of the Union, the states, the Federal District or the municipalities.

The texts of literary, artistic or scientific works.
Lectures, addresses, sermons, and other works of the same nature.
Dramatic and dramatic-musical works.
Choreographic and pantomimic works, whose scenic performance is fixed in writing or in any other way.
Musical compositions, whether or not they have lyrics.
Audiovisual works, with or without sound, including cinematographic works.
Photographic works and those produced by any process analogous to photography.
The works of drawing, painting, engraving, sculpture, lithography and kinetic art.
The illustrations, geographical maps and other works of the same nature.
The projects, sketches and plastic works concerning geography, engineering, topography, architecture, landscaping, scenography and science.
Adaptations, translations and other transformations of original works, presented as a new intellectual creation.
Computer programs.
Collections or compilations, anthologies, encyclopedias, dictionaries, databases and other works which, by their selection, organization or arrangement of their content, constitute an intellectual creation.

In the case of computer programs, specifically, §1 of this article establishes that they are still the subject of a specific law: Law 9,609, of February 19, 1998.

On the other hand, art. 8 of Law 9,610 establishes which works are not protected by this law:

The ideas, normative procedures, systems, methods, projects or mathematical concepts as such.
The schemes, plans, or rules for carrying out mental acts, games, or business.
Blank forms to be filled in for any type of information, scientific or otherwise, and their instructions.
The texts of treaties or conventions, laws, decrees, regulations, judicial decisions and other official acts.
Commonly used information, such as calendars, agendas, entries or captions.
The isolated names and titles.
The industrial or commercial use of the ideas contained in the works.

According to the law, the author of a work will always be the individual who generated it, not the legal entity. Protection to legal entities may, however, also be granted in cases provided for by law. This just does not apply to computer programs, which, according to Law 9,609, are the exclusive property of the producing company and not of the programmers hired by it.

According to art. 46 of Law 9,610, reproduction does not constitute an offense against copyright:
In the daily or periodical press, news or informative article, published in newspapers or periodicals, with the mention of the author's name, if signed, and the publication from which they were transcribed.
In diaries or periodicals, of speeches given at public meetings of any nature.
Of portraits or any other form of representation of the image, made to order, when performed by the owner of the ordered object, with no opposition from the person represented therein or his heirs.
Of literary, artistic or scientific works, for the exclusive use of the visually impaired, whenever the reproduction,

without commercial purposes, is done using the Braille system or any other procedure in any support for these recipients.

From a single copy of small excerpts, for the private use of the copyist, provided that it is made by him, with no intention of profit.

The citation in books, newspapers, magazines or any other means of communication, of passages of any work, for purposes of study, criticism or controversy, to the extent justified for the purpose to be achieved, indicating the name of the author and the origin of the constructions.

From the collection of lessons in educational establishments by those to whom they are addressed, their publication, in whole or in part, without prior and express authorization from the person who taught them being prohibited.

Of literary, artistic or scientific works, phonograms and radio and television broadcasting in commercial establishments, exclusively for demonstration to customers, provided that these establishments sell the supports or equipment that allow their use.

Theatrical performance and musical performance, when performed in the family recess or, for exclusively didactic purposes, in educational establishments, with no intention of profit.

From literary, artistic or scientific works to reproduce judicial or administrative evidence.

Of small excerpts, in any works, of pre-existing works of any nature, or of an entire work, in the case of plastic arts, provided that the reproduction itself is not the main objective of the new work and that it does not harm the normal exploitation of the reproduced work nor cause unjustified prejudice to the legitimate interests of the authors.

Therefore, the rule is to copy only the essentials of other works, as long as it is really necessary to put information about these works or draw a comparison, always remembering that the copied excerpt must appear in quotation marks and with a citation of the source so that there is never any doubt about it. whether or not it is plagiarism.

Plagiarism in Brazil is considered a crime, and the law provides for a fine and imprisonment. Therefore, it is not worth transgressing this law. There is also no more serious or less serious plagiarism. Plagiarism is a crime under the law, and academically it is a very serious ethical fault. There was a case where a student plagiarized only the methodological procedures chapter of his monograph, copying it from another monograph (actual case). He actually did the work, did the research, got the data and generated the conclusions. But, due to the lack of ethics of having copied part of the work, this student had his diploma revoked, regardless of other factors.

12.4 Pearls of Plagiarism

Augusto CB Areal presented on his website a series of comments by plagiarists, which are pearls that show the type of reasoning or ignorance that is often behind this type of attitude. The material is no longer online, but some of these pearls obtained in 2009 are transcribed below to illustrate:

"[...] you should be proud to see your work in a great success that is not the case of your page[sic]." The plagiarist can't even write correctly...

"[...] which in no way constitutes the action mentioned in the subject (subject) of your email, which refers to the crime of coercion using a white or firearm to obtain property alien. An accusation, moreover, that may well be the subject of legal proceedings for slander and defamation (considering that several people have a testimonial copy of their criminal offense) [sic]." Here, the plagiarist accuses the author of defamation, since he would have said that he had his material stolen, when, in fact, it was stolen.

"I thought you would be proud." No comments.

"If you don't want anyone to copy it, don't put it on the Internet. It's silly to think that there will be exclusivity on the content on the Internet. Pure bullshit [...] that's the Internet, man. The correct way to deal with the situation is not to talk about [...] copyright law, but to relax and enjoy while the internet is still ours [...]." Under this logic, if you don't want someone to steal your car, don't go out with it.

"I found your abortion about plagiarism on the net super interesting, however, I found that on your page there are some gifs (images) that I think are not your authorship. It would be better if they were removed, because it is contradictory to talk about plagiarism and do the same, even if they are public domain gifs[sic]." Well, if it's in the public domain, you can use it, right?

Regarding the use of materials in the public domain or with the author's authorization, care should only be taken to verify that the person authorizing the use is really the author. There are cases of sites that appropriate third-party materials and authorize their use by other people, but would not have the right to do so.

12.5 Ethics in Article Submission

When submitting one or more articles to conferences or journals, the author must be aware of the ethical aspects considered by the scientific community.

Another aspect that is not so evident, but also important, is that an article, even if it has not yet been published, must be submitted to only one vehicle at a time. That is, one should not be tempted to send the same article to several events at the same time, in the hope that one of them will accept it. Snyder (1993) points out that "simultaneous submission without notice is considered highly unethical".[1]

Some conferences and journals even accept simultaneous submission to another vehicle, as long as they are explicitly informed.

The correct way of trying to publish is, therefore, to send a first version of the article to a vehicle and wait for the result. Being approved for publication, great! Otherwise, the evaluators will send a list of reasons together with the information on the refusal to publish. This list will contain suggestions for improving the work, which can be used by the author in order to improve the article before sending it to another vehicle.

Yet another aspect to be considered is the case of publishing two or more similar articles on the same subject. It is not ethical to make multiple versions of the same article and send them to different outlets. Each article features one or more research ideas that were evaluated. Thus, articles, even if different in form, that present the same ideas, are considered a form of self-plagiarism and, therefore, unethical. It is possible, on the other hand, to publish several articles from the same research work, provided that each one deals with different aspects of the work, that is, each article must explore a different research idea or, in the case of older publications, you can generate a new article deepening or extending the results already presented.

It is not possible to directly copy the text of an article already published in another, even in the case of the author himself. Once the text has been published, it can be cited in a new article by means of a bibliographic reference, in quotation marks, as if it were any other text. Each article must therefore be written with predominantly original text.

The only exception to this rule is the reuse of the monograph text in a scientific article. It is considered natural that the monograph may originate one or more articles and, therefore, copying parts of the author's own monograph in these articles is not considered plagiarism. Translation: "Simultaneous submissions without warning are considered highly unethical."

Requirement Levels

Depending on the level of the course, the degree of requirement in relation to the completion work should vary. Although Eco (1989) defines the monograph as text with 100-400 pages, size is not document. What is evaluated is the degree and type of contribution that the student has made in the work.

The structure of Brazilian higher education identifies different types of courses. Initially, undergraduate courses, which can be taken by high school graduates. There are several types and modalities: Bachelor's, Engineering and Licentiate are considered full undergraduate courses. Faster undergraduate courses are technology courses, which form the technologist, and sequential courses, which are even faster.

Graduate courses are characterized by two types of courses: lato sensu and stricto sensu. The lato sensu courses, usually called "specialization" or, following North American fads, MBA (Master in Business Administration), are of a more technical nature and complement professional technical training.

The stricto sensu courses, in their two levels, master's and doctoral degrees, seek to train higher education researchers and professors. These are courses, therefore, with very different characteristics from undergraduate and lato sensu courses.

There is also, in Brazil, the professional master's degree, which seeks to train a researcher in an area very close to professional application. It is not a compromise between specialization and a scientific master's degree.

It is simply a different way of conceiving a master's course, with direct application of the knowledge generated in a specific professional area. The requirements in terms of scientific contribution in the academic and professional masters are usually the same.

In general, just having an undergraduate degree is enough to be able to enter a master's program. To enter the master's degree, it is not necessary to have a specialization, although sometimes this can enhance the candidate's curriculum in the selection process. Certain universities also validate some courses taken at a specialization level for students who enter the master's degree. It must be verified case by case how the university proceeds in this validation.

The doctorate is considered the full and definitive degree in academic terms. The title of PhD is nothing more than a doctorate obtained in an English-speaking country (Eco, 1989).

There are other equivalent titles abroad as well, and care must sometimes be taken not to confuse them with titles granted in Brazil. For example, there are countries in Europe with one-year master's courses, in which the student only takes courses and delivers a written work, basically consisting of a bibliographic review. These courses are not considered equivalent to the Brazilian master's degree, but rather to specialization courses.

For a diploma abroad to be recognized in Brazilian territory, it must be revalidated by a Brazilian university delegated by the Ministry of Education for that purpose (in general, federal universities). No matter how highly regarded the diploma obtained abroad is, it will only be valid in Brazil through this revalidation process. This process is, in most cases, time-consuming, as the Brazilian university that has a stricto sensu program in the area of the monograph presented will constitute an evaluation panel that will verify if the work would have the quality to be approved in the program itself. Having quality, the title is revalidated and receives a stamp on the back of the diploma, attesting to its validity in Brazil. Otherwise, the request is refused.

In the case of distance learning courses, it must be verified, initially, if the institution has express authorization from the Ministry of Education to offer this type of course. In the case of foreign institutions that offer distance learning courses in Brazil, special care must also be taken, as the diploma is issued abroad and is not automatically valid here.

Postdoc is not an academic title. Usually, researchers with recent doctorates do an internship carrying out research for 6 to 24 months with a more experienced researcher at another institution. But this relationship does not generate a degree and, therefore, is not an academic degree. The main result expected from a post-doctorate is the production of scientific articles and the maturity of the researcher who submits to them, in addition to the strengthening of the bond of cooperation with the institution visited.

13.1 Graduation

What do you expect from an undergraduate thesis? At this level, two types of course completion work can be done: technological and scientific. Scientific work must follow the methodological lines described in this book.

Technological work, on the other hand, usually consists of the student being able to show that he knows how to apply the techniques he has learned throughout the course. The development of an interesting system can be a good example of end-of-course work, as long as the student develops it using techniques learned during the course and presents a report showing this.

However, even if the student is only going to develop a product, it can be very important for him to do a systematic mapping to find out which products already exist and in which his product may be different. Suppose, for example, that the student would like to develop a computerized sprint backlog tool. Before starting to analyze requirements or write code, he should research which tools already exist and what their characteristics are. Thus, he will then be able to create a better one than the existing ones because he has characteristics that they do not have. He is not generating science, because the work does not generate new knowledge, his product is a computer tool. But this tool can become relevant in the market if it discovers its unique characteristics.

13.2 Specialization

Specialization courses have already been seen as a step towards reaching the master's degree. Today, however, they are seen much more as a professional complement or update. Under Brazilian law, every specialization course requires the preparation and public defense of a monograph.

This monograph can even be a research work, done in the methodological molds presented in this book. But it is also acceptable, in many courses, for the student to develop only a bibliographic study and present the ideas learned with some small personal contribution, usually consisting of comments on the bibliography or the results of simple experiments. In general, in these cases, proof of hypotheses or a more relevant scientific contribution is not required. This, however, varies greatly from course to course. The student must be aware of the requirements placed by the course in which he is enrolled.

The specialization student will then be able to make good use of systematic literature reviews and will be able to formulate exploratory, descriptive or cause-effect questions to obtain some personal contribution to the area.

13.3 Master's and Doctorate

Most of the recommendations in this book apply to master's and doctoral degrees. In both cases, the student is expected to make a contribution to science that is relevant, that is, that is not trivial, that is useful and that is correct.

The difference between what is expected in the master's and in the doctorate resides more in the level of requirement of the contribution than in the form. In both cases, the application of scientific methodology is required, the comparison with related works, the elaboration of a research hypothesis and its confirmation or refutation. The difference then lies in the expected impact of this contribution.

For the Master's, in general, it is enough for the student to present new information on a topic that is relevant to the area. In the case of a doctorate, this new information has to be important enough to change the way people view that area of research. In other words, the doctorate is expected to produce a contribution that actually changes the state of the art.

Furthermore, a thesis must be "original" and "substantial". It is often difficult to assess this. It is up to the advisors, with their experience, to guide the students in order to choose an objective that is compatible with the level of the course they are obtaining.

The difference between the master's and the doctorate is not in the form of the document or in the presentation, but in the depth and difficulty of the problem to be addressed. A doctoral thesis requires solving a more difficult problem and, consequently, more significant contributions.